The Personal Finance Guide for Tech Professionals

Building, Protecting, and Transferring Your Wealth

Tom Taulli

Apress®

The Personal Finance Guide for Tech Professionals: Building, Protecting, and Transferring Your Wealth

Tom Taulli
Monrovia, CA, USA

ISBN-13 (pbk): 978-1-4842-8241-0   ISBN-13 (electronic): 978-1-4842-8242-7
https://doi.org/10.1007/978-1-4842-8242-7

Managing Director, Apress Media LLC: Welmoed Spahr
Acquisitions Editor: Shiva Ramachandran
Development Editor: James Markham
Coordinating Editor: Jessica Vakili

Distributed to the book trade worldwide by Springer Science+Business Media New York, 1 New York Plaza, New York, NY 10004. Phone 1-800-SPRINGER, fax (201) 348-4505, e-mail orders-ny@springer-sbm.com, or visit www.springeronline.com. Apress Media, LLC is a California LLC and the sole member (owner) is Springer Science + Business Media Finance Inc (SSBM Finance Inc). SSBM Finance Inc is a **Delaware** corporation.

For information on translations, please e-mail booktranslations@springernature.com; for reprint, paperback, or audio rights, please e-mail bookpermissions@springernature.com.

Apress titles may be purchased in bulk for academic, corporate, or promotional use. eBook versions and licenses are also available for most titles. For more information, reference our Print and eBook Bulk Sales web page at http://www.apress.com/bulk-sales.

Printed on acid-free paper

Table of Contents

About the Author

Tom Taulli, a published author and a software developer, is also an Enrolled Agent, the highest certification with the IRS that allows him to represent taxpayers before the agency. He is also the owner and co-founder of Pathway Tax, which he started over 20 years ago. The focus is on helping clients with tax preparation, planning, and resolution.

Tom has also written columns for online publications such as BusinessWeek.com, TechWeb.com, and Bloomberg.com. You can reach Tom on Twitter (@ttaulli) or through his website (PathwayTax.com).

Introduction

As I write this Introduction, the stock market has suffered a major decline. True, this has come after a long bull run. But it certainly does not make investors feel any better. Bear markets are awful.

They are also a wake-up call. They highlight the importance of diversification. They also show the importance of taking a holistic approach to your personal finances. This means taking into account insurance, tax planning, and estate planning.

And this is what my book is about. It's not just about the various investments you can put your money in. The goal is to provide a comprehensive approach.

The issues for tech professionals can be particularly complex. The bear market, for example, has hit tech stocks the hardest. There are also the issues of dealing with equity compensation, like stock options. There is the risk of having too much of your wealth in shares of a few companies. When working with startups, the planning for benefits, such as for health insurance, can be challenging.

Now this is not to make you depressed! The tech world is exciting. There are many secular changes that will propel growth. But it is still important to build a good financial foundation. This will help you get through the occasional downturns.

OK then, so what about my background? Most of my career has been in the tech industry, since the early 1990s. I founded several companies and raised venture capital. Along the way, I got firsthand experience with unique personal finance issues and situations.

To better understand these, I took a tax course and then got my license as an Enrolled Agent. This is the highest designation of the IRS (Internal Revenue Service) and allows me to represent people before the agency.

In 2002, I started my own tax and financial advisory firm, called PathwayTax.com. I have helped many tech clients. A big part of this has been with tax preparation and planning. But I have also helped people resolve their tax problems, such as with back taxes and unfiled returns.

I've also done quite a bit of writing on financial and tax matters. I've written for publications like Forbes, Barron's, Kiplinger, Motley Fool, and BusinessWeek.

Disclaimer

So before starting with this book, I want to provide a disclaimer. Keep in mind that I will not be providing personalized legal, accounting, or other professional services or advice. This course is meant to be educational in nature. My recommendation is for you to seek out qualified professionals when it comes to doing things like putting together a financial plan or preparing your tax returns. This will definitely be worth the money.

So why write this book? The main reason is that I have worked with many tech clients with their equity compensation. This has meant handling complex financial and tax issues. I also have clients who have come to me after they made mistakes with their tax returns and received notices from the IRS. Thus, the goal of this book is to provide the reader with a basic foundation of the essential personal finance issues and strategies for tech employees.

www.wsj.com/articles/tech-giants-turn-to-a-classic-recruitment-tool-cash-11645957980?mod=hp_lead_pos2

CHAPTER 1

Stocks and Bonds

The Core Investments

> *How many millionaires do you know who have become wealthy by investing in savings accounts? I rest my case.*
>
> —Robert Allen, finance author[1]

You can boil investments into two flavors: debt and equity. Debt is where you loan money to earn interest. Then after a period of time, you will get your initial loan amount back.

As for a stock, you will buy shares in a company. The money will go to either of the following:

- Directly to the company. This can be through an angel investment, venture capital, or an initial public offering (IPO).

- To another investor who sells the stock.

---

[1] www.goodreads.com/author/quotes/25187.Robert_G_Allen

© Tom Taulli 2022
T. Taulli, *The Personal Finance Guide for Tech Professionals*,
https://doi.org/10.1007/978-1-4842-8242-7_1

Regardless, you will own a fraction of the company and will benefit if the stock price increases or there is a dividend paid. History has shown that this is one of the best investments for building wealth.

True, these examples are simplistic. But when looking at investments, it's a good idea to understand the fundamentals. There can be many extraneous details that can make it much more difficult to analyze the potential returns and risks.

In this chapter, we'll take a look at the two main ways to invest – that is, with stocks and bonds.

The Basics of Stocks

A stock represents ownership in a company and is a mechanism to raise capital. For example, suppose you launch a startup, called Cool Corp., and a friend is willing to invest $25,000 in the new venture. You incorporate your business and establish the total number of shares at 1,000,000. But you will not issue all of these because you want enough for future rounds of funding or for employee stock options. Instead, you set aside 100,000 of the shares for the initial capitalization of the company and come up with a price-per-share of $1 – which puts the valuation at $100,000. You get 80,000 shares or 80% of the stock and the remaining 20% goes to your investor.

A key advantage of having a corporation is that it has limited liability. The reason is that the law considers the organization to be a "person." It can enter into contracts, own assets, take on liabilities, and even be sued.

Why is this important? The owners of the stock are only liable for their investment. That is, if you invested $1,000 in Cool Corp., then this is your total liability exposure. Period. Your personal assets are not subject to forfeiture, say if there is a lawsuit.

In our Cool Corp. example, the company is a privately held business. This is the most common form in the United States. According to the Kaiser Family Foundation, there are over 6.2 million privately held businesses in the United States.[2]

A much smaller number of companies are publicly held. This is where their shares are traded on an exchange like the New York Stock Exchange or NASDAQ. There are about 6,000 publicly traded companies in the United States.[3] To be listed on an exchange, a company usually needs $100 million in annual revenues or will hit this level within a couple years. There should also be a defensible business and a large market opportunity.

If a company cannot meet the requirements, it may list on the OTCQB. Various foreign companies, like Tencent Holdings and Roche Holding AG, are on the platform. There are also many penny stocks, which generally sell below $1 a share. Then there are stocks that were delisted from the NYSE or NASDAQ that failed to meet the requirements.

These securities can be extremely volatile and there are periodic frauds and scams. From 2011 to 2020, the average annual return of the US listings was −44%, according to the analysis of Sihan Zhang.[4]

---

[2] https://bit.ly/32tMT3T

[3] www.marketwatch.com/story/the-number-of-companies-publicly-traded-in-the-us-is-shrinkingor-is-it-2020-10-30

[4] www.wsj.com/articles/crypto-boom-retail-investors-fuel-rise-in-over-the-counter-stock-trading-11633339981

Note   A common scam with penny stocks is the "pump and dump." Promoters will use a corporate shell – which has few assets – and leverage social media and other channels to create excitement about the stock. Often this is about focusing on a hot trend. Then when the stock price soars, the promoters will unload their holdings. The stock price will eventually plunge. Interestingly enough, Hollywood has highlighted the "pump and dump" in films like *Boiler Room* and the *Wolf of Wall Street*.

The Securities and Exchange Commission has taken actions to improve the quality of the market. This has included a requirement that a company must be current with its financials in order to have its stock price quoted on brokerage systems. Financial firms like Schwab and Fidelity have also implemented their own systems to help avoid problems with clients.

Whether a company is privately held or publicly traded, the shareholders have certain rights. You can vote on important matters of the corporation, such as for the nomination of directors, mergers, and the liquidation of the firm. The directors are a small group of people that meet periodically to make decisions on matters like setting executive salaries, hiring executives, establishing dividend payments, and helping with the strategic direction of the company.

Note   When it comes to voting, it's about "one share, one vote." But some stocks have different classes. This is to allow the founders or investors to have voting control. For example, Facebook founder and CEO, Mark Zuckerberg, has Class B shares that have 10 votes for each share. As for the Class A shares, each one has one vote. So even though Zuckerberg owns less than 10% of Facebook, he has about 60% voting rights.

Shareholder votes usually happen at a company's annual meeting. But if a person cannot attend, they can vote by proxy. This is a document you can fill out and deliver to the company via mail or a website.

Here are some of the other rights of shareholders:

- Dividends: If a board declares a payment, then the shareholders have a right to it. A dividend is usually in cash, but sometimes it can be in the form of more stock. A dividend is also usually for mature companies that have consistent cash flows, and the payments are often made every quarter.

- Inspection rights: A shareholder can get access to documents like the bylaws and board meeting minutes.

- Securities laws: The state and federal governments have extensive regulations on stocks. These generally focus on providing disclosures to shareholders, such as with the risk factors, financials, and business plan.

- Lawsuits: Shareholders can bring suits against a company, such as for fraud and concealment. These legal actions are mostly for large companies.

How to Make Money with Stocks

As noted above, one of the ways to make money with stocks is through dividends. This may mean getting 1% to 4% on your initial investment. However, the higher return often comes from capital gains, which is when the price of the stock increases.

Then what drives the value of a stock? There are a myriad of factors to consider:

- News: The launch of a product, a major deal, or an acquisition are just some of the items that can make an impact. A company's earnings report is another big one. Although, even if a company shows strong growth, this may not be enough. The price of a stock is generally based on expectations for a company. If the earnings fall below these, its typical for the stock price to fall.

- Macro Factors: The growth in the economy and changes in interest rates can have a significant impact on stocks. The same goes for events like wars and yes, pandemics.

- Manias: This is when investors get overly enthusiastic about certain stocks or sectors. Examples include the late 1990s dot-com boom and the meme mania in 2001, which saw the skyrocketing of stocks like GameStop and AMC. Manias can certainly generate substantial returns, but they can deflate quickly.

- Industry Trends: This is often about changes in technology. Examples include the emergence of the smartphone, cloud computing, and artificial intelligence. But industry trends may result from changes in beliefs. This has been the case with the focus on ESG (Environmental, Social, and Governance) investing.

- Profit: This is ultimately the main long-term factor for a stock's value. Profit is an indication that there is a real need for a company's products or services. This also allows for more capital to invest in the operations, pay dividends, and buy back stock.

Next, you can use short selling, which allows you to make money when the value of a stock falls. In fact, short selling is often blamed for problems in the market and some people even consider it to be immoral.

But in any market, there is the ability to engage in short selling. It actually helps to provide for a smoother functioning of trading. Interestingly enough, when short selling has been banned, it often does not reduce the volatility.

So how does short selling work? Let's take an example. Suppose you research the prospects of ABC Corp. and believe that they look particularly bad. The stock is currently trading at $50, which you think is way overvalued. For the short sale, you will borrow 100 shares of ABC Corp. from your stock brokerage account and then sell them. This will put $5,000 into your account.

Within a few months, ABC Corp. stock sinks to $20 and you decide to take your profit. To close out the trade, you purchase 100 shares for $2,000 and then return them to the brokerage account. Your profit is $3,000 or the $5,000 from the initial short sale transaction minus the $2,000 purchase of the shares.

Short selling can be risky. Basically, the maximum return is limited to the initial value of your purchase. This would be the case if the stock price goes to zero, which is highly unlikely. In our example, this would give you a $5,000 profit.

On the other hand, there is really no limit to how high the stock price can go. If ABC Corp. stock goes to $100, then you would have a loss of $95,000. The is $100,000 – which is the value you buy back the shares for – minus the $5,000 you have in your account.

Note   In 2020, some of the world's top investors lost substantial amounts because of their short sales of Tesla stock. The estimate from S3 Partners is over $40 billion.[5]

Common vs. Preferred Stock

There are two main flavors of stock: common and preferred stock. As the name implies, common stock is the most prevalent. As mentioned earlier in this chapter, you have certain rights and the potential to receive dividends.

Preferred stock, on the other hand, does not provide for voting rights. But there are certain advantages when compared to common stock, including the following:

- Priority: In the event of a liquidation of the company, the preferred stockholders get any of the proceeds ahead of the common stockholders. There is also priority of the dividend. That is, the company must pay the preferred stockholders first.

- Dividend: This is usually a fixed percentage of the par value. For example, if the preferred stock is $100 per share and the dividend rate is 5%, then you will get $5 every year. The payment is usually made on a quarterly basis. Also, if a company misses dividend payments, these must be paid first – ahead of those for the common stockholders – if the dividend is resumed.

---

[5] www.cnn.com/2021/01/06/investing/tesla-shorts-losses-elon-musk-win/index.html

- Call: This allows the company to buy back the preferred stock. The price is usually at a premium to the par value.

Warren Buffett is someone who is a big fan of preferred stock. During the financial crisis, he lent money to various companies using this type of security. One case was with Bank of America. Buffett invested $5 billion in preferred stock that had a 6% annual dividend, amounting to $300 million. As part of the deal, he got a warrant. This allowed him to purchase 700 million common shares of Bank of America at $7.14 each. In 2017, when the company's shares were fetching $24.32, he exercised his warrant and then exchanged his preferred stock for common stock. As a result, his paper gain was $12 billion and he became the largest shareholder in Bank of America.[6]

Venture capitalists also typically use preferred stock for their financings. However, this type of security is usually different than for publicly-traded preferreds.

Note   An American Depository Receipt (ADR) is stock of a foreign company that trades on a US exchange. A bank handles the paperwork, such as with the filings, custody of the shares, and the currency transactions. But an ADR trades like any other stock.

---

[6]www.cnbc.com/2017/06/30/warren-buffett-just-made-a-quick-12-billion-on-bank-of-america.html

Risks of Stocks

The long-term returns for stocks are definitely compelling. From 1970 to 2020, the average gain was 12.19%, based on data from MoneyChimp. com.[7] If you invested $10,000 in 1970 in the S&P 500 and held onto your shares, your portfolio would have reached an impressive $1.8 million.

Yet the markets can plunge. If the drop is 10% to 19%, it is considered a correction. Anything more than this is called a bear market.

Here are some notable examples:

- 1930–1932: −83%

- 1973–1974: −48%

- 2007–2009: −57%

Note   The term "bull market" comes from how the animal attacks – that is, it uses its horns in upward moves. As for a "bear market," this describes how a bear uses its paws to strike downward.

In such times, it can be extremely tough to keep faith with the stock market. But history has shown that this is the right approach.

When it comes to the risks of an individual stock, though, they are much greater. Even seemingly great companies can falter and suffer long-term declines. Just look at GE. From 2000 to 2021, the shares dropped from $440 to $100. Again, this is why it is important to diversify your investments.

---

[7]www.moneychimp.com/features/market_cagr.htm

The biggest risk for a stock is bankruptcy. When this happens, the owners of common stock are last in line to get proceeds from the liquidation – and there is usually nothing left. This is why the bankruptcies of companies like Borders Books, Pets.com, Blockbuster Video, and Enron saw their stock prices dive to zero.

Stock Analysis

In 2019, writers at the *Wall Street Journal* put together an experiment. They threw darts at a list of stocks and compared them to the picks of top investors at the Sohn Investment Conference. The bottom line: the dart throwers posted returns of 27% higher. Only 3 of the 12 professional investors outperformed the S&P 500.[8]

Yes, investing in stocks is far from easy. This is why there is so much popularity in focusing on funds that invest in the market indexes.

Regardless, many people still try to find winning investments – and some of them do quite well. This has been the case with investors like Warren Buffett, George Soros, Carl Icahn, Peter Lynch, Bill Ackman – just to name a few.

There are a myriad of strategies and approaches to picking stocks. But here are the two main ones:

- Fundamental Analysis: This is where an investor will analyze the company's prospects for its revenues and profits. This can include researching the financial statements, understanding industry trends, analyzing the economy, and evaluating competitive advantages.

---

[8] www.marketwatch.com/story/random-darts-beat-hedge-fund-stars-again-2019-06-26

- Technical Analysis: This involves looking at patterns on a chart, such as the price movements and changes in the volume. This can be a way to detect momentum in a stock.

Buying and Selling Stock

It's easy to buy and sell stocks, especially for those listed on exchanges. You will setup a brokerage account, which can take 15 to 20 minutes. You will fill out information about your background as well as fund the account, such as by linking to your bank. Of course, you can also write a check or make a wire transfer.

When you make a transaction, you will specify the name of the company or the ticker (this is an abbreviation, which can be from one to four letters). You can then specify the type of order:

- Market Order: This means you will place the order at or very near the current stock price.

- Limit Order: You will specify the price for the order. When it hits this level or is at a better price, the trade will be executed.

- Stop-Loss Order: When a certain price is hit, then a market order will be issued. This is often a way to help protect gains. For example, suppose you purchased ABC Corp. at $10 and the price goes to $25. You then set a stop-loss order at $20. If the price hits $20 or below, a market order will be automatically triggered.

The settlement of a trade is the process where the stock is bought or sold, and the cash is transferred. This is based on T+2 (trade date plus two days). That is, the settlement happens two days after the day you make the trade.

Note   If you buy fewer than 100 shares, then this is called an odd lot. If the amount is 100 or is evenly divisible by 100, then it's a round lot. So, a transaction for 100 shares or 500 shares is a round lot. Then what about when a transaction is greater than 100 but not evenly divisible by 100? This is a mixed lot.

You can also purchase fractional shares. This is when you buy shares based on the dollar amount. For example, suppose you have $1,000 and you want to buy Amazon stock, which trades for $3,200. In this case, you can buy 0.3125 of the share. Many brokers do not charge commissions on these transactions and the fractional share can be as low as 0.001 and the purchase amount of $0.01.

If a stock pays dividends, you will get the fractional share. But you will not get voting rights on these shares.

The Basics of Options

There is often confusion with stock options. First of all, these investments can be complicated. Next, stock options that you buy from your broker are not the same that you will receive from your employer. Instead, these are employee stock options and we'll cover these in Chapter 10.

During the past few years, investing in stock options has become extremely popular. In 2021, the trading volume reached record highs and much of the growth has been from individual investors.[9]

There are two kinds of options. First, there is a call option, which gives you the right to buy 100 shares of a stock at a fixed price for a period of time, say three months.

---

[9]www.barrons.com/articles/stock-options-day-trading-market-51637349456?mod=hp_LEAD_1

Here's an example: Suppose you are interested in the prospects of Microsoft and the stock is currently trading at $100. If you purchased 100 shares, then you would pay $10,000.

But you then look at a stock option. It has a strike price of $100 and the premium is $5. This means you would pay $500 for the call option ($5 premium multiplied by 100 shares). If the stock price increases by $2, then your premium will be worth $7 per share or $700 – for a return of 40%. However, if you purchased the 100 shares outright for $10,000, then your return would have been only $200 ($2 multiplied by 100 shares) or 2% ($200 return divided by the $10,000 investment).

So the option sounds pretty good, right? It does in this example. Basically, with an option, you get the power of leverage. You are only using a fraction of the investment to play the swings in the stock.

However, the reality is that many options expire worthless. For example, suppose that by the end of three months, Microsoft stock is trading back at $100. In this case, the option would go to zero. After all, why would anyone pay money for an option that allows you to buy Microsoft for $100 when you can do this in the open market?

Note that a premium has two main drivers of value:

- Intrinsic Value: This is the current price of the stock minus the strike price. In our Microsoft example, let's say that the price of the shares are $104 at the time of expiration. This means that the intrinsic value is $4 ($104 market price minus the strike price of $100) and the option is considered to be in-the-money.

- Time Value: This is the value based on the expectations of investors for the price of the stock. Let's continue with our Microsoft example. Let's say the option has two months left until expiration and the stock price is $102. As for the strike price, it is $100 and this translates into an intrinsic value of $2 per share or $200. But what

if the premium is $600? The additional $400 is the time
value of the call option. For the most part, investors
think the value of the shares will keep on climbing.

It's important to note that the time value will generally decline until
expiration. There will be less and less time for the stock to have a big move.
Instead, the intrinsic value will become more of the value of the option –
assuming it is in-the-money.

Then how does a put option work? It allows you to make money when
the stock price falls. You can sell 100 shares of a stock at a fixed price for a
period of time.

Suppose that you think this will be the case with ABC Corp. The
current stock price is $10 and the put option has a strike price of $10. The
premium is currently at $3 per share or $300.

In a few weeks, ABC Corp. falls to $7 per share and the premium is now
at $5. The premium has a time value of $2 and an intrinsic value of $3 (or
$10 strike price minus $7 market price).

A put option is not just for purposes of speculating on the potential
for a drop in the stock price. You can also use it as a way to protect your
gains. For example, suppose you bought XYZ Corp. for $10 and it soars to
$30. But you are concerned about the overall market and buy a put that
has a strike price of $25. If XYZ stock starts to fall, the premium on the put
should increase – and this should help offset the losses.

You can also use a put option on market indexes. In other words, this
can be a hedge against your portfolio of stocks.

Writing Options

There are two sides to an option. We've already seen that the buyer of the
option pays for the premium. Then there is the option writer or seller. This
person will create the option and sell it.

The writing of a call can be covered – which means that you own the underlying shares – or naked. Let's look at the first type. Suppose you own 100 shares of IBM and they trade at $100 each. If you think the stock will trade flat or increase moderately for the next few months, then you might consider a covered call. This can actually provide you with some income. If the premium is $2, then you will get $200.

Assume you sell a covered call on your IBM stock and the strike price is $115. The option is currently out-of-the money since the strike price is above the market value. Here's a look at some scenarios:

- IBM increases to $120 when the option expires: You are required to sell your 100 shares for $115 or a total of $11,500. Your gain is $1,500 (the $11,500 sale minus the value when you wrote the call, which was $10,000 or $100 multiplied by 100 shares). You also include the $200 premium for a total of $1,700. Basically, the covered call means that your maximum gain is the difference of market price and the strike price plus the premium. You then miss out on anything above this.

- IBM increases to $115 at expiration: Because this is at the strike price, the call options has zero value. Your gain is the maximum, which is $1,700.

- IBM declines to $95 at expiration: The call option has no value since the strike price is above the market price. On the 100 shares you own, you sustain a loss of $500, which is $9,500 ($95 multiplied by 100) shares minus $10,000 ($100 multiplied by 100, which is the value at the time you wrote the call).

In a way, writing covered calls is a more conservative approach to options. If the stock falls, the premium you received helps to soften the loss. Or, if the stock stays flat or increases slightly, then the premium represents income. For some investors, they will periodically use covered calls to generate ongoing income – so long as the holdings remain relatively stable.

Although, a riskier approach is an uncovered call, which is when you do not own the underlying shares. The maximum you can make is the premium. This is so long as the stock stays flat or declines.

The problem is that the losses can be much larger. Assume you write an uncovered call on 100 shares of XYZ Corp. and the stock price is $10. The premium is $200.

Then by expiration, the stock shoots up to $25. In this case, you will have a loss of $1,200, which is the $200 premium plus the $1,000 (100 shares multiplied by $10) minus $2,500 ($25 multiplied by 100 shares).

Let's now look at how to write a put. You do this on ABC Corp, whose stock is selling at $20 and the strike price on the put is $15. The premium is $2 or $200. By doing this, you are agreeing to buy the stock if it falls below the strike price. This is why the brokerage firm will want to make sure you have enough money or assets in your account to make this trade.

Here are some of the scenarios:

- ABC Corp. stock rises to $25 at expiration: The option will be worthless and your gain will be the $200 premium.

- ABC Corp. stock drops to $10 at expiration: You will be required to buy 100 shares at the strike price for a total of $1,500. Unfortunately, this means your position is at a loss of $500. But the $200 premium will lessen the impact.

Keep in mind that there are many types of option strategies – and they can be quite intricate. Some have colorful names like married puts, bull call spreads, long straddles, long call butterfly spreads, and so on. They also range in terms of risks and potential returns. Although, for purposes of this book, the focus is on the basic strategies. If you want to learn more about options, there are a variety of helpful online resources:

- Investopedia (`https://www.investopedia.com/`)

- Tastytrade's YouTube Channel (`https://www.youtube.com/channel/UCLJiSMXJ9K-1AOTqIqdXJgQ`)

Other Terms and Concepts About Stocks

Here's a look at various other terms when it comes to stocks:

- Public Float: This is the number of shares that are traded on a stock exchange. For an IPO, this is usually a relatively small amount. The reason is that many of the employees, executives, and venture investors have stock that has sale restrictions. Because of this, the price swings can be more volatile since it does not take as many share purchases or sales to move the price. Although, over time, the float will increase because of increases in sales.

- Capitalization or Market Cap: This is the value of a company, which is calculated by multiplying the stock price by the number of shares outstanding. Investors will often classify stocks based on capitalization. A typical range is $300 million to $2 billion for a small cap company and $2 billion to $10 billion for a mid-cap company. Anything higher would be a large cap company and a capitalization lower than $300 is called a micro-cap company. In some cases, a mega cap is where the value is over $200 billion.

- Pink Sheets: These are small companies that are not traded on a national exchange. Rather, the shares are on the over-the-counter market, which usually has less liquidity and access to financial information. Often shares on these markets are known as penny stocks.

- Stock Split: In some cases, the price of a stock can get to a high level, say over $100 a share. Companies may split the stock to make it more affordable for smaller investors. This is done by issuing more shares. For instance, in a 2-for-1 stock split, the company will increase the number of shares outstanding by 100%. But since there has been no fundamental change in the company's fortunes, the stock price will fall by 50%.

- Reverse Split: A stock may sink to low levels, such as under $1. A stock exchange may actually delist the company's shares because of this. What to do? A company may execute a reverse split. This will reduce the number of shares outstanding so as to boost the stock price. Thus, if there is a 1-for-2 stock split, the company will reduce the number by 50% and this will increase the stock price by 100%. But like the case with a stock split, there is no change in the overall value of the stock.

- Price-to-Earnings Ratio (PE Ratio): This is a way to gauge the value of a company. It is calculated as the price of the stock divided by the earnings per share (EPS) for the year. A low PE ratio is generally 10–15, while a high one is over 20. For the most part, a company will have a higher multiple if there are strong growth prospects.

- Total Return: This is the capital gains for the stock plus the dividends.

- 10-K: This is the annual financial statement for a company.

- 10-Q: This is the quarterly financial report for a company.

- Cyclical Stock: This is a company that tends to perform quite well when the economy is in the upswing, but decelerates significantly when the economy falters. Examples of such companies include airlines and steel operators.

- Defensive Stock: This is a company that generates steady growth whether the economy is doing well or not. Examples of such companies include utilities and food producers.

The Basics of Bonds

A bond is a loan that usually has an interest payment and a maturity date, which is when the loan needs to be paid back. The biggest issuers of bonds include governments and large companies. Companies often use bonds to finance large capital projects, such as to buy a company, acquire assets, or even to buy back more shares. As for governments, they will use bonds to finance their spending for items like social programs, defense, and infrastructure.

The interest payment on the bond is usually fixed. But it is becoming more common for floating rate payments, which adjust to changes in interest rates.

Let's take an example of a bond transaction: ABC Corp. is growing quickly and needs to build a new plant. This will cost $300 million, such as to purchase the land, buy the equipment and materials, and hire the construction workers. ABC Corp. hires a Wall Street firm to manage the bond financing. The firm creates an offering to sell 300,000 bonds at $1,000 each (this is the par or face value) and the annual interest rate will be 4%. The maturity will be in ten years.

If you buy one of these bonds, then you will get $40 in interest every year (4% multiplied by $1,000), which is usually paid twice a year and is called the coupon rate. Then after ten years, you will get your $1,000 back. However, until this time, you can sell your bonds in the open market – which may have a higher or lower price than the $1,000. This depends on interest rates or changes in the fundamentals of the company.

The Rewards and Risks of Bonds

We've already seen one way to make money from bonds is to earn interest. This can certainly be a steady stream of income. However, with interest rates at historically low levels, this has not been much of a benefit.

But you can make money when the price of the bond rises. How does this work? The main reason has to do with the following concept: there is an inverse relationship between interest rates and the price of a bond.

To see how this works, let's continue with our example of ABC Corp. If interest rates in the economy remain the same, then the bond will trade at about $1,000. But of course, interest rates tend to move. Suppose the Federal Reserve takes actions to ease monetary policy and this drives down interest rates. This is mainly because of heavy purchases of bonds, which drive up the prices.

Let's say that similar bonds to ABC Corp. are now offering 3.8%. But since your own bond has a coupon of 4%, you can sell it at a higher price. This could be at about $1,030 (note that this is a very rough estimate and will depend on other factors like the maturity). For the new buyer, the yield will be 3.8% or $40 divided by $1,030.

On the other hand, if interest rates rise, then the price of your bond will fall. Suppose that interest on equivalent ABC Corp.'s bonds are at 4.20%. The price on the bond will be at $950.

There may be times when a bond will increase or decrease in value regardless of the movements in interest rates. This is largely due to changes in the prospects of the organization that owes the debt. If there is an inability to pay the interest or face value of the bonds, then the prices can plunge. On the other hand, if an organization improves its prospects and its ability to meet its commitments become more favorable, then the prices will likely improve.

To evaluate this, many bonds have ratings from third-party research companies like Standard and Poor's, Moody's, and Fitch Ratings. They have professional analysts that evaluate the financials and industry trends.

The bond ratings have two different tiers: investment grade and non-investment grade. For investment grade, the highest is called Prime, which is designated as AAA for S&P and Aaa for Moody's. Only two US companies have this rating: Microsoft and Johnson & Johnson.

Then there are different levels of ratings from High Grade to Lower Medium Grade. The range is AA+ to BBB− for S&P and Aa1 to Baa3 for Moody's.

As for the non-investment grade ratings, these are for higher risk securities. They are often called "speculative-grade," "high-yield" or "junk bonds." They usually have higher interest rates because of the potential for default.

The range of the ratings is from BB+ to D (this is for when the bond is in default) for S&P and Ba1 to C for Moody's.

If there is a default and a bankruptcy filing for a company, there will be a priority of claims for the different types of bonds. For those that are secured, they will get paid first. Then there are unsecured bonds. These debt holders have a general claim to the assets after the secured bonds have been paid off. There are also a priority of claims for the unsecured bonds, which include

- Senior unsecured debt

- Senior subordinated debt

- Subordinated debt

- Junior subordinated debt

By the time of a bankruptcy, the owners of the bonds will usually be hedge fund investors that specialize in distressed debt. An example of this is chronicled in the book by Max Frumes and Sujeet Indap called *The Caesars Palace Coup*. It is about the bankruptcy of Caesars, which had about $18 billion in debt.[10] Billionaire investors Howard Markets from Oaktree Capital and David Tepper of Appaloosa Management owned junior subordinated debt. Because of strong negotiating tactics and key legal rulings, they were able to snag 66 cents on the dollar for their bonds. They were originally offered 9 cents on the dollar.

Now when it comes to bonds, there are definitely other risks to consider:

- Inflation Risk: If the interest rate is fixed on a bond, then inflation will mean lower returns. The reason is that the purchasing power of the interest payments will be less over time. This will also be the case with the face value of the bond.

---

[10] www.reuters.com/article/us-usa-caesars-breakingviews/breakingviews-review-when-oceans-eleven-meets-chapter-11-idUSKBN2BB161

- Reinvestment Risk: Some bonds have a call feature, which allows the company or government to buy them back. This is usually for a refinancing. That is, if interest rates fall, then the bonds will be replaced with those with lower coupons. The problem for investors is that they will get their money back and then be left with similar bonds that have lower rates.

- Duration: Bonds with longer maturities are more susceptible to risks of inflation, interest rate moves, and potential default. Because of this, the rates are usually higher.

- Liquidity Risk: For some bonds, there may not be many buyers and sellers. In other words, it could mean having to take a larger cut in the price when you want to make a sale.

In terms of the historical returns of bonds, they generally lag those on stocks. According to Forbes Advisor, the return was 5.59% since the Great Depression of the 1930s.[11] Yet this is not to imply that investors should avoid bonds. They are a critical part of portfolio diversification. After all, when stocks do not perform well, bonds may do the opposite – and also provide steadier streams of income.

How to Buy and Sell Bonds

A bond can cost $1,000 to $5,000. This can be difficult for many investors, as there are no fractional purchases. Another difficulty is that there is often little investment research – at least compared to stocks.

---

[11] www.forbes.com/advisor/investing/stock-and-bond-returns/

Although, if you want to purchase a Treasury bond, the minimum is only $100. This is if you buy it from the TreasuryDirect website (https://www.treasurydirect.gov/) and there are no commissions or fees involved.

You can also purchase bonds through a broker like E*TRADE, Fidelity, Schwab, and so on. This could be for a public offering or a transaction on the open market. Keep in mind that only a small number of bonds are traded on exchanges like the NYSE. The rest are on the OTC (Over-the-Counter) market, which is where buyers and sellers transact with brokers or dealers.

How do brokers make money from bond transactions? They are called mark-ups, which means that the commission is factored into the price you pay for the bond. For example, a brokerage may buy a bond at $1,000 and sell it to you for $1,015. Interestingly enough, a broker may not even disclose this.

The mark-up can have a significant impact on the return of your bond. According to Fidelity, a $15 charge can reduce your yield-to-maturity from 3% to 2.83% on a ten-year bond.

As a result, it's a good idea to shop different brokers and ask them for clear disclosures on their mark-ups.

Types of Bonds

There are many types of bonds available. You can also buy those that are short-term (with maturities under two years), medium (two to ten years) and long-term bonds (some can have maturities of 100 years).

Then there are bonds that do not even have coupons. Yes, these are called zero coupon bonds. With this security, the interest is implied because it is sold at a deep discount to the face value. A common one is a Treasury bill.

Here's an example of a zero coupon bond. A Treasury bond has a maturity of five years and a face value of $1,000. The interest rate is 5% and it is compounded semi-annually (this means the interest is computed twice a year). This means that the price of the bond will be $781.20.

The interest is considered to be imputed each month. Although, even though you do not receive any cash payments for this, the IRS will still actually deem this to be income. In other words, you will pay taxes on the imputed interest. Because of this, zero coupon bonds are usually for tax-advantage accounts like IRAs (Individual Retirement Accounts).

OK then, so in the next few sections, we'll review the main types of government bonds.

Federal Government Bonds

The US government is the world's largest borrower. This is done primarily through the issuance of bonds by the US Treasury (they are often called Treasuries). There are different types based on the maturity:

- Bills or T-Bills: These are zero-coupon bonds that have maturities of a few days, four weeks, 13 weeks, 26 weeks, and 52 weeks.

- Notes or T-Notes: These come due in two, three, five, seven, and ten years. Financial institutions often use the rate on T-Notes for determining the interest on mortgages, car loans, student loans, and so on.

- Bonds: The maturities are 20 and 30 years.

There are also federal government bonds that have special features. They include the following:

- Treasury Inflation-Protected Securities (TIPS): These bonds adjust the face value based on changes in the Consumer Price Index (CPI), which measures inflation in the economy. The maturities are five, ten, and 30 years.

- Floating Rate Notes (FRNs): These are bonds where the coupon varies based on the movements of the 13-week Treasury bill. The maturity is two years and the interest is paid quarterly.

The market for government bonds is highly liquid. There are over 20 primary dealers in these securities that are ready to trade. The interest on Treasuries is subject to federal income tax but not state and local income taxes.

Federal government bonds are very safe. They are backed by the "full faith and credit" of the US government. Basically, it has the power not only to levy taxes but even print money to pay the debt obligations. Although, because of this security, federal government bonds generally have lower rates.

Note that federal government agencies can issue their own bonds and there are two types. One includes federal government agency bonds, which have the "full faith and credit" backing. The common agencies include the Federal Housing Administration (FHA), Government National Mortgage Association (GNMA), and the Small Business Administration (SBA).

Next, there are government-sponsored enterprise (GSE) bonds. While these are quite safe, they do not have the direct backing of the US government. Because of this, the rates tend to be higher. Some of the GSE organizations are the Federal Farm Credit Banks Funding Corporation, Federal National Mortgage Association (Fannie Mae), and Federal Home Loan Mortgage (Freddie Mac).

Note   Treasury bonds can give a false sense of safety. Suppose you buy a bond with a 2% yield. Then within the year, interest rates rise by 1%. This would mean a 20% drop in the price of the bond. When you factor in the 2% yield on your bond, your annual return would be −18%.

Municipal Bonds

States, cities, and counties issue municipal bonds. They are usually for funding major projects, such as highways, bridges, hospitals, and schools.

A key benefit for investors is that the interest is tax exempt from federal, state, and local taxes. This is so long as the investor is a resident of where the bond was issued. Although, depending on your income, interest on municipal bonds may be subject to the alternative minimum tax.

Note   Because of the tax benefits of municipal bonds, these securities usually have lower rates than other bonds. There is often higher demand when it looks like the federal government or state expects to raise taxes.

Some municipal bonds are also taxable. This is where the federal government will not subsidize the project because there is not a significant public benefit. Examples include bonds to finance stadiums, housing backed by private investors, refinancing of debt, or an underfunded pension plan.

Municipal bonds can have different terms, such as from 1 to 30 years. There are also three main categories:

- General Obligation (GO) Bonds: These are for projects that do not generate revenues, like parks. These bonds are also backed by the "full faith and credit" of the municipality. Because of this, the interest tends to be lower. After all, the municipality can raise taxes to pay the interest.

- Revenue Bonds: These are bonds where the funding is based on the revenues generated by the project. Some are non-recourse, which means that if the revenue stream disappears, there will be no other means to fund the bond.

- Conduit Bonds: This is where the municipality will issue the bond on behalf of a private organization, like a nonprofit college, housing project, or hospital. The private organization will be liable for the payment of interest and principal. If there is a default, the municipality is not on the hook.

Defaults on municipal bonds are rare. Based on a study from Fidelity, the default rate – on five-year securities – was only 0.13% from 2010 to 2019.[12] By comparison, the default rate for corporate bonds was 6.3%.

A famous municipal bond default came in the summer of 2019. The city of Detroit declared bankruptcy and suspended payment on billions of dollars of general obligation bonds. In the end, investors received 14 cents to 75 cents on the dollar.[13]

---

[12] www.fidelity.com/bin-public/060_www_fidelity_com/documents/fixed-income/moodys-investors-service-data-report-us-municipal-bond.pdf
[13] www.thebalance.com/municipal-bonds-what-are-they-and-how-do-they-work-3305607

Junk Bonds or High-Yield Bonds

As we saw earlier, junk bonds or high-yield bonds do not have investment-grade credit ratings. But this does not mean they are bad investments. Generally, investors get higher interest rates on these bonds to compensate for the risks. Consider the Markit iBoxx USD Liquid High Yield Index, which is a popular way to measure the performance of junk bonds (there are over 1,300 securities in the index). From 2011 to 2021, their average return was 6.65%.[14]

Junk bonds can certainly be volatile though. While interest rates are a major factor in the price movements, a company's prospects are also critical. In fact, some junk bonds often perform more like a stock.

A company's bonds may actually start as investment-grade and then drop to junk status because of a deterioration of the business. This type of security is called a fallen angel bond. An example is Ford. Because of the impact of the Covid-19 pandemic in 2020, the company's bonds were downgraded to junk status.

Convertible Bonds

A company will issue convertible bonds to raise capital. The interest rates are usually lower since investors can convert their bonds into a fixed number of shares.

For example, suppose ABC issues convertible bonds that mature in five years and have an annual coupon of 3%. The conversion ratio is 20 or the $1,000 par value divided $50 per share. Thus, if ABC stock sells over $50, it would make sense to convert the bond into shares.

---

[14] www.ishares.com/us/products/239565/ishares-iboxx-high-yield-corporate-bond-etf

In a way, this security provides the benefits of both a bond and stock. If the stock price underperforms, you still receive the ongoing interest payments. You also will get the par value repaid at maturity or if the bond is called. Basically, this provides downside protection.

Then again, if the stock price performs well, you get the benefit of this when you make the conversion or sell the convertible bond in the open market.

Note   Convertible bonds have become quite popular for tech companies. These securities often provide a low-cost of capital. In 2021, companies like Airbnb, Expedia, and Coinbase issued convertible bonds that had zero interest.[15]

Conclusion

In this chapter, we got a look at the two main types of investments. Stocks provide the potential for strong returns, but also can be quite volatile. There are also stock options that can magnify the returns or even lower other risks.

Bonds, on the other hand, are more stable. There are also some bonds, like municipals, that provide for tax advantages.

Then there are hybrid securities that have elements of both stocks and bonds. Examples include preferred stocks and convertible bonds.

In the next chapter, we'll take a look at mutual funds and exchange-traded funds (ETFs).

---

[15] www.wsj.com/articles/convertible-bond-sales-are-soaring-in-2021often-at-0-interest-11622199601

CHAPTER 2

Mutual Funds and ETFs

An Easier Way to Invest

> *If you have the stomach for stocks, but neither the time nor the inclination to do the homework, invest in equity mutual funds.*[1]
>
> —Peter Lynch, former portfolio manager

Investing is similar to baseball. The fact is that you will have lots of strikeouts, foul balls, and fly outs. This is the case for the newbie investors to the world's best.

Just look at Warren Buffett. In an article for CNBC.com, he set forth 15 of his biggest investing regrets.[2] He recounted some companies that suffered huge losses. But Buffett also recounted examples where he should have made investments, such as for Google and Amazon.com.

---

[1] www.inspiringquotes.us/topic/8474-mutual-fund

[2] www.cnbc.com/2017/12/15/warren-buffetts-failures-15-investing-mistakes-he-regrets.html

© Tom Taulli 2022
T. Taulli, *The Personal Finance Guide for Tech Professionals*,
https://doi.org/10.1007/978-1-4842-8242-7_2

Regardless, he still has racked up one of the best track records ever. As of the end of 2021, Warren Buffett was worth a staggering $107 billion, ranking him No. 8 on the Forbes list.[3]

True, few people have his investment acumen. But this is not required to make strong returns. The good news is that there are many mutual funds and exchange-traded funds (ETFs) that allow you to benefit from the efforts of professional managers.

Let's take a look.

The Basics of Mutual Funds

A mutual fund pools money from a large number of investors. The fund's portfolio managers will then invest in stocks, bonds, or other assets. Usually, there will be a charter for the objectives of the mutual fund, such as the following:

- Growth stocks

- Dividend-paying stocks

- Foreign stocks

- Government bonds

- Junk bonds

According to Statista, there were about 7,600 mutual funds in the United States in 2020.[4] A large number are actively managed, which means that portfolio managers select the investments. The other funds are passive. This means that the investments are based on the movements of an index like the S&P 500.

---

[3] www.forbes.com/profile/warren-buffett/?sh=434b65004639

[4] www.statista.com/statistics/255590/number-of-mutual-fund-companies-in-the-united-states/

The price of a mutual fund is called the net asset value or NAV. It's calculated as

(Current market value of all the investments – liabilities) / total number of shares

For example, ABC Growth fund has $100 million in assets. The fund calculates this at the end of trading each day, which is 4:00 pm (eastern standard time). There are also liabilities of $5 million and 50 million shares outstanding. The NAV would then be $1.90, which is $95 million ($100 million in assets minus $5 million in liabilities) divided by 50 million shares.

Some of the advantages of mutual funds are

- Professional Management: The portfolio managers usually have finance educations, certifications, and experience. Some of them have become near celebrities like Sir John Templeton, John Neff, Bill Miller, and Peter Lynch.

- Diversification: A typical fund will have over 100 investments in the portfolio. So, while some of the investments will likely fall, others will offset the losses.

- Affordability: Most mutual funds have small minimum investment requirements. Some are as low as $50.

Note   Some mutual fund companies, like T. Rowe Price and Fidelity, invest in private companies. When these companies go public, the investments can generate substantial gains. Although, according to federal regulations, mutual funds can invest up to 10% of their assets in private companies.[5]

---

[5] www.wsj.com/articles/more-mutual-funds-are-pumping-money-into-small-firms-1493604240

How to Make Money with Mutual Funds

There are different ways to make money from mutual funds. First of all, there is the increase in the NAV, which reflects the overall gains in the portfolio. Next, you are entitled to your pro rata share of any dividends and interest generated from the mutual fund's investments. Federal law requires that these must be paid at least once a year in the form of a dividend. However, for mutual funds that invest in bonds or dividend-paying stocks, the payments can be quarterly or even monthly. There is also a reinvestment feature, in which you can buy more shares of the mutual fund with your dividends. But you will still be subject to taxes on these amounts.

Then there are capital gains distributions. These are usually for the end of the year, and when a mutual fund has generated significant gains by selling the investments. But for investors, this can be a surprise and it may mean paying higher taxes. So before buying a mutual fund, look to see if there will be a capital gains distribution. This is also considered a short-term capital gain, which is taxed at your ordinary rates. This is usually higher than if you received a long-term capital gain. This is why it is popular to place mutual funds in tax-advantaged vehicles like Individual Retirement Accounts (IRAs) and 401(k)s. There will be no taxes on the capital gains distributions, dividends, or sales of the mutual funds so long as the investments are not withdrawn.

How to Buy and Sell Mutual Funds

You can buy shares in a mutual fund directly from the mutual fund itself. You can either call the firm, have an office visit, or set up an account through the website. You can also buy shares from a mutual fund from a brokerage, bank, or other financial services firm.

When you make a purchase, it will be for the NAV on the next business day. And when you want to sell, this depends on what firm your shares are held. If they are with the mutual fund, then the firm will buy them directly. This is called a redemption. But if you have shares with a financial company, then you will sell through their own system.

When you purchase shares in a mutual fund, the mutual fund will create new shares. Then when you sell the shares, the redemption will eliminate the shares. This is why a mutual fund is called an open-end fund.

Many mutual funds allow you to set up purchase programs. For example, you can buy $100 of shares each month. You can also indicate to reinvest all dividends and capital gains.

If you buy your mutual fund through a financial advisor, then you may be charged a commission, which is known as a load. It can be levied when you make a purchase (front-end loads) or when the shares are sold (back-end loads or contingent deferred sales charges or CDSCs).

Note   If you do your own research for a mutual fund, then you should select a no-load fund.

But there are a myriad of other potential fees:

- Redemption Fee: This is a fee the mutual fund charges when you redeem shares. The limit is 2% of the NAV. This fee is usually to discourage short-term trading, say with trades within 30 days.

- Exchange Fee: This is a fee a mutual fund charges if there is a transfer of funds to another fund within the fund group.

- Account Fee: This is a fee for an account when the value is less than a certain level.

- 12b-1 Fee: This is for the mutual fund to pay for marketing, distribution, and shareholder services. The maximum is 1% of the NAV.

The expense ratio is the amount of the fund operating expenses divided by the NAV. They usually range from 0.25% to 1.5%. The operating costs include the expenses for the portfolio managers, any 12b-1 fees, legal services, accounting, administrative costs, and so on.

The Basics of ETFs

ETFs (exchange-traded funds) are a recent phenomenon. The first one hit the markets in 1993, which was the SPDR S&P 500 ETF Trust or SPY ETF. It tracked the performance of the S&P 500 (this includes the top large cap and midcap stocks in the United States). At first, the index got off to a slow start. But once investors saw the benefits of the ETF, the demand accelerated.

Today the SPY ETF is the largest, with over $440 billion in assets.[6] ETFs are also the fastest growing category of funds. The total assets are over $9 trillion – a doubling since 2018 – and there are over 2,000 funds.[7]

ETFs have similarities with mutual funds. Both pool investor funds and provide for diversification. They also have the NAV to value the shares.

Then again, there are some major differences. Perhaps the biggest is that an ETF is a stock – which has a ticker symbol – that is traded on an exchange like the NYSE or NASDAQ.

---

[6]www.ssga.com/us/en/intermediary/etfs/funds/spdr-sp-500-etf-trust-spy
[7]www.wsj.com/articles/global-etf-assets-hit-9-trillion-11628769548

Here are some other differences:

- You can short sell shares or borrow against their value with a brokerage margin account.

- You can buy fractional shares. In other words, there are no minimum investment requirements.

- You can use different transaction types, like limit and stop orders.

This flexibility is certainly a big advantage compared to mutual funds. Although, since an ETF is a stock, the settlement for trades is two days, which compares to one day for a mutual fund.

It's true that some ETFs have annual capital gains distributions. But they are usually less than those for mutual funds. Some of the reasons include less selling of securities in the portfolio and how the shares are created and redeemed.

ETFs actually have two prices. As noted, the NAV measures the value of the portfolio, and this is done continuously throughout the trading day. But the ETF itself will have its own price and this is what you will use to buy or sell the security. The two prices often diverge, but usually not by significant amounts. Large investors will often use sophisticated trading systems to make profits on the differentials, which helps to narrow the spreads.

ETFs usually are based on indexes. An index is used to measure the performance of a market. Some of the common ones are

- Dow Jones Industrial Average (DJIA): Charles Dow and Edward Jones created this in 1896 (they would go on to launch the Wall Street Journal). It tracked the 12 top stocks on the NYSE and the first index value was 40.94. Eventually, the Dow expanded to 30 stocks and the types of companies included have evolved as the economy has changed. For example, the index has tech companies like Microsoft, Intel, Salesforce.com, Apple, and Cisco.

- S&P 500: Standard & Poor's launched this in 1957 and it quickly became a proxy for the US stock market. The index covers 11 industry sectors, and a committee periodically changes the companies.

- CRSP (Center for Research in Security Prices) US Total Market Index: Developed at the University of Chicago, the index covers close to 4,000 stocks. This is essentially the whole market for investable equity in the United States. Vanguard uses the index for its mutual funds and ETFs for the Vanguard Total Stock Market Index Fund, which represents 10% of the market.[8]

- Russell 2000 Index: This tracks the performance of the 2,000 smallest publicly traded companies.

- Nasdaq-100 Index: This is for the 100 largest non-financial US companies.

- Bloomberg Barclays US Aggregate Bond Index: This tracks most US traded bonds.

- Morgan Stanley Capital Investments (MSCI) Indexes: These include a myriad of indexes to track foreign markets.

There are two ways to calculate an index. First, there is the price-weighted index, which is less common. This is where the prices of the stocks are added up and then divided by the number of stocks. However, with stock splits and changes in the index, the divisor will change over time. This has been the case with the Dow Jones Industrial, which is a price-weighted index.

---

[8]www.wsj.com/articles/mutual-funds-that-ate-wall-st-11638390382?mod=hp_lead_pos9

Next, there is the capitalization-weighted index, such as the S&P 500. This is where companies that have larger market capitalizations – like Apple or Microsoft – will have more impact on the value of the index.

So why the popularity for using indexes? This approach – which is often called passive investing – is based on a very important fact. Portfolio managers often fail to beat the markets. This is especially the case with equity funds. According to Morningstar, only 25% beat out passive funds during a ten-year span.[9]

Then again, the timing of the market is far from easy. It means predicting complex factors like fiscal and monetary policy, understanding industry trends, and analyzing the prospects for many companies.

Consider Bill Miller. From 1991 to 2005, his Legg Mason Value Equity Strategy beat the S&P 500. It was the longest streak ever recorded. However, after this impressive performance, the fund generally underperformed. Then there was the 55% plunge during 2008. As a result, the fund saw a spike in withdrawals.

Despite all this, Bill Miller remains one of history's best portfolio managers. He also was not a market timer. Instead, he focused on the long-term growth prospects of his investments. In a quarterly report, he noted: "[s]ince no one has privileged access to the future, forecasting the market is a waste of time. It is more useful to try and understand what is happening now and give up trying to predict what is going to happen."[10]

---

[9] www.cnbc.com/2021/11/01/in-one-of-the-most-volatile-markets-in-decades-active-fund-managers-underperformed-again.html
[10] https://millervalue.com/bill-miller-3q-2021-market-letter/

Two of Miller's biggest investments were Amazon and bitcoin. He owned Amazon for over 20 years and became the third largest holder, behind Jeff Bezos and his ex-wife, MacKenzie Scott. As for bitcoin, Miller purchased the digital currency when it was trading between $200 to $300.[11] During the end of 2021, it was trading for over $50,000.

Now another key reason for the growth in passive investing is the low costs. After all, there is no need to hire high-priced portfolio managers. The investment selection is generally based on using automation systems. There are usually less transaction costs because there is not as much buying and selling. The reason is that most indexes do not change frequently.

As a result, the expense ratio of an ETF can be as low as 0.10% to 0.20% of the NAV. In some cases, it is actually at zero.

The difference of a 1% expense ratio of an actively managed fund may not seem like much compared to a 0.10% level for a passive fund. But this can add up over the long term. For example, if you invest in a mutual fund that has an average return of 5%, the passively managed firm will grow to $26,032 in 20 years while the actively managed fund will go to $21,911.

Note   ETFs do not have loads. But there may be commissions on the stock trades. If you have a financial planner, they may also charge a fee for the ETFs and mutual funds in your account.

There is also a strong academic underpinning to passive investing. It's called the Efficient Market Hypothesis or EMH. The pioneer of this theory is Eugene Fama, who is a finance professor at the University of Chicago. During the 1960s and 1970s, he wrote pathbreaking papers on

---

[11] https://markets.businessinsider.com/news/stocks/stock-market-outlook-bill-miller-fairly-valued-bitcoin-open-question-2021-7

the EMH. They essentially indicated that stocks and other investments factored in all available information. Thus, investors really had no edge. However, Fama did acknowledge that there were outliers that beat the markets. But this was mostly a statistical fluke.

The EMH became a huge driver in the growth of passive investing. During the 1980s, pensions and endowments saw this as a way to deal with the lackluster returns on their portfolios. Then in the 1990s, passive investing started to become popular with individual investors.

Yet there are criticisms of EMH. Professor Robert Shiller noted that it was "one of the most remarkable errors in the history of economic thought." His research has shown that – over longer periods of time – EMH has proven less impactful.[12]

Some markets are also generally less efficient. This is where there is not as much research coverage and trading activity. Examples of these markets include bonds, real estate, and foreign securities.

But the bottom line is: The research is fairly convincing that passive investing is a smart approach. This is especially the case for those funds that have lower costs.

The Drawbacks of ETFs

ETFs are far from perfect, of course. With the surge of interest, there are many firms jumping in. A growing trend is to convert actively managed mutual funds into ETFs. This is not particularly bad. But it may mean that the expenses are much higher. This means it is important to do your research.

---

[12] www.wsj.com/articles/SB10001424052702303680404579139530872119634

There are also other issues with ETFs, such as the following:

- Tracking Errors: The management of an ETF can be complicated. One of the biggest difficulties is tracking the index. In some cases, there may be divergences with the price of the ETF. In this situation, you may suffer from lagging returns.

- Leveraged ETFs: These use sophisticated strategies to try to magnify the returns. For example, a 2X ETF will increase 2% for every increase in the index. While this can supercharge the returns, this can also mean that the losses can be substantial. Note: There are also 3X ETFs.

- Closure: An ETF may ultimately close down. This is usually because of the performance or the lack of investor interest in a particular investment niche. If an ETF closes, you will not lose your money. But it will likely mean that the investment lagged.

- Liquidity: Some markets have less trading activity. This can mean that the costs are higher because there are larger spreads between the bid and ask prices of securities. An example is the municipal bond market. There are over 50,000 state and local governments that sell this type of debt.[13] But liquidity became an issue when the Covid-19 pandemic hit. Many investors simply did not want to buy or sell the bonds – and this made it difficult to value the ETFs.

---

[13] www.wsj.com/articles/etfs-claim-more-of-muni-market-11640212153?mod=hp_lead_pos6

- Actively Managed ETFs: These could mean increased volatility. An example is the ARK Investment Management, which has an assortment of ETFs that focus on high-growth tech companies. The CEO of the firm is Cathie Wood, who has quickly become a rising star in investment world. But after a couple years of standout returns, her funds took a major hit in 2021.[14] Some of the portfolio holdings – Zoom, DocuSign, Robinhood Markets, and Teledoc – have suffered losses of over 50%.

Another growing issue with ETFs is concentration risk, which is especially the case with large cap funds. The reason has been the surge in the megatech names like Apple, Microsoft, Tesla, Facebook, and so on. In 2021, the top ten companies represented 30% of the value of the S&P.[15]

True, there is still lots of diversification among the other stocks. And the top ten companies are certainly high-quality.

On the other hand, history has shown that stocks can easily go out-of-favor – and for prolonged periods of times. After all, during the 1990s, Apple nearly went bust. Then from 2000 to 2014, Microsoft stock was flat.

Now this is not to say to avoid the S&P 500. But when putting together your portfolio, you need to understand its components and the risks. For example, if you already have lots of exposure to the top ten names, you may then want to have a lesser weighting for an investment in the S&P 500.

---

[14] www.wsj.com/articles/cathie-woods-ark-innovation-etf-sinks-during-selloff-11638561092

[15] www.wsj.com/articles/gigantic-stocks-are-a-reason-to-worry-11640530981

> **Note**   During the 1960s and 1970s, there was a group of stocks called the "Nifty 50." They were also known as "one decision stocks" because they were blue-chip operators like Coca-Cola, General Electric, and IBM. But they would ultimately fetch stratospheric valuations. Then in the 1973–1974 bear market, these shares plunged and many of them would not rebound until the 1980s. The "Nifty 50" craze became a classic example of how valuations matter when it comes to investing.

ESG (Environmental, Social, and Governance) Investing

BlackRock is the world's largest money manager firm, with nearly $10 trillion in assets.[16] The firm operates a large number of mutual funds and ETFs.

As should be no surprise, BlackRock CEO Larry Fink is certainly influential. In his annual letter for 2021, he shook up the financial world by writing about ESG (environmental, social, and governance). This is where companies and investors should be mindful of climate change, diversity, and gender relations.

---

[16]www.wsj.com/articles/blackrock-profit-rose-23-in-third-quarter-11634122455

In the letter, Fink pushed to have companies disclose how they were reducing greenhouse-gas emissions. He also indicated that his firm would be more aggressive with its share voting for ESG issues and even sell companies that were not doing enough. According to Fink: "The more your company can show its purpose in delivering value to its customers, its employees, and its communities, the better able you will be to compete and deliver long-term, durable profits for shareholders."[17]

And yes, BlackRock has followed up with this by launching its own ESG funds. The firm has the ambitious goal of growing this part of its business to $1 trillion by 2030.[18]

Note   ESG investing is not new. It has been around for decades. One of the pioneers of the category is Calvert Research and Management, which launched in 1976. At the time, the investment category was called "socially responsible investing." Calvert was the first money management firm to oppose Apartheid in South Africa.

The typical ESG fund is based on an index like the S&P 500. However, there will be exclusions of certain companies. But there are also funds that focus on certain sectors like solar or cleantech.

Some funds will also play the futures markets that track carbon credits. This is where countries or regions set up emissions limits and those firms that cannot meet them will need to purchase offsets.

---

[17] www.blackrock.com/corporate/investor-relations/larry-fink-ceo-letter
[18] www.wsj.com/articles/blackrocks-fink-urges-companies-to-disclose-do-more-on-greenhouse-gas-emissions-11611670619

A fund in this category is the KraneShares Global Carbon Strategy ETF. According to the firm: "The index introduces a new measure for hedging risk and going long the price of carbon while supporting responsible investing."[19]

The market for carbon credits is estimated at over $260 billion.[20] The major segments include European Union Allowances (EUA), California Carbon Allowances (CCA), and the Regional Greenhouse Gas Initiative (RGGI).

Note   Schroders, which is an asset management firm, conducted a survey of over 23,000 persons from 32 locations across the globe. About 47% of the people indicated that they were interested in sustainable investments.[21]

ESG investments have their challenges. One of the biggest is that there is no global standard. For example, could an ESG investment be a nuclear power plant? For some people the answer would be "yes." Nuclear energy provides substantial power and does not produce carbon emissions. Then again, others would argue that there is the problem of disposing nuclear waste as well as the possibility of an accident.

Some ESG funds will actually invest in traditional oil companies. This may sound strange, but it does make sense. The reason is that some of these companies are cutting back aggressively in their carbon emissions. An example is Royal Dutch Shell. The company expects to reduce its

---

[19] https://kraneshares.com/krbn/

[20] https://kraneshares.com/krbn/

[21] www.schroders.com/en/us/private-investor/insights/global-investor-study/2020-findings/sustainability/

carbon emissions by 50% by 2030. Royal Dutch Shell is also lowering its oil production and has invested more in alternative energy. By 2050, the company forecasts it will reduce its carbon level output 100%.[22]

Next, when it comes to ESG investing, investors may be more interested in environmental issues versus social concerns. And what about the "G" for governance? This appears to be a confusing part of ESG investing. Governance is about how companies handle compliance, the composition of the board of directors, and the abilities of the management team.

Because of this, there are some financial firms that set up separate accounts. This allows clients to have more discretion of what investments to make. But this is primarily for wealthy persons. Yet in the years ahead, it seems likely that there will be more affordable customization options. This could ultimately be about investors creating their own ETFs.

Another issue with ESG investments is "greenwashing." This is where the fund uses claims that are not based on the facts.

To combat this, governments are also looking at ways to promote standards for disclosures. The European Union has been at the forefront of this trend. It has drafted rules – called Sustainable Finance Disclosure Regulation, or SFDR – for asset managers for their disclosures of ESG messages. There is also another set of standards for publicly traded and large private companies.

In the United States, the Securities and Exchange Commission is looking at ways to enforce better transparency. But this is still in the early phases.

Finally, ESG may ultimately not turn out to generate strong returns. This could mean not reaching your financial goals. One survey shows that ESG funds have expense ratios that are near 6X those of passive funds.[23]

---

[22] www.wsj.com/articles/shell-aims-to-halve-emissions-by-2030-as-activist-calls-for-breakup-11635410997
[23] www.wsj.com/articles/esg-investing-in-five-years-11637161312?mod=ig_esgreport

Closed-End Funds

Closed-end funds are one of the first types of funds for individual investors. They emerged in the late 1890s and focused primarily on investments for railroads. They would remain popular until mutual funds emerged in the 1920s.

As of today, closed-end funds have kept a similar structure. The fund is "closed" because after the initial capital is raised – through an IPO – there are no inflows or outflows from investors. The money will then often be invested in bonds and the interest will be paid as dividends either monthly, quarterly, or biannually.

Shares of a closed-end fund are traded on national exchanges. You can have limit and stop orders. You can also short sell the shares.

It's common for the price of a closed-end fund to trade at a discount to the NAV. As a result, some investors will buy shares when the divergence is large and then make a profit when the spread shortens. In fact, sometimes the portfolio managers of the closed-end fund will buy back shares so as to boost the stock price.

There is also the ability to borrow against the assets. This can help to boost the returns – so long as the investments do well. But then again, if there is a fall off, the losses can accelerate. Although, when it comes to closed-end funds, the risks of these transactions are generally well calculated.

For the most part, there are a fairly small number of closed-end funds. The fact is that mutual funds and ETFs get much of the attention.

Direct Indexing

Direct indexing is where you purchase the investments in an index directly. This has usually been for institutions and wealthy investors that want more flexibility with their passive investing. Such investments have been done primarily with separate accounts.

But direct indexing is becoming more mainstream. Some of the reasons include commission-free stock trading and fractional shares. Keep in mind that roboadvisors like Wealthfront have their own offerings and large asset managers like Vanguard and BlackRock are investing in the category.

The main reason for direct indexing is taxes. Since you own the shares directly, you can sell your losers and use these to deduct against your gains. This process is known as "tax harvesting." In other cases, an investor may want to donate or gift the stocks.

According to a study from Professor Terry Burnham, indirect investing generated better after-tax returns of 1.08% compared to a portfolio that was static. This was based on data from 1926 to 2018.[24]

Indirect investing uses sophisticated software to identify the potential tax advantages. It will also replicate an index with fewer investments. For example, it's possible to get similar returns on the S&P 500 with less than 100 stocks. The software will also rebalance the portfolio when there are changes to the index or sales of stocks.

Another advantage of direct indexing is portfolio customization. If you want to exclude investments for ESG purposes, you can easily do this. Or suppose you work at a company like Nvidia or Apple and have a large holding of the shares. You can exclude the stock from the index, which can help to lower your concentration risk.

---

[24] www.wsj.com/articles/pros-and-cons-of-direct-indexing-11638 390453?mod=hp_jr_pos1

There are some downsides. Consider that the fees can be much higher than typical index funds. They range from 0.30% to 0.40%.[25]

Another problem is that the sales may result in material differences with the index. This may ultimately mean underperforming the benchmark. What's more, losing stocks can make big comebacks. But with direct indexing, you could miss out on these opportunities.

Conclusion

Mutual funds and ETFs provide an easy and affordable way to build diversified portfolios. But interestingly enough, one of the key factors for performance is low costs. This is why investing in passive funds has become so popular. Besides, it's common for actively managed funds to underperform their benchmarks.

Returns are not necessarily the only goals for investors. More and more of them are looking to ESG factors. The good news is that there are many mutual funds and ETFs to choose from in the sector. But you need to do your research since some of them make claims that are misleading.

Finally, ETFs and mutual funds can be inflexible. This is why there are emerging approaches like direct indexing to allow sophisticated tax strategies and portfolio customization.

In the next chapter, we'll take a look at alternative investments.

---

[25]www.wsj.com/articles/pros-and-cons-of-direct-indexing-11638 390453?mod=hp_jr_pos1

CHAPTER 3

Alternative Investments

Going Beyond Stocks and Bonds

> *It's not whether you're right or wrong that's important, but how much money you make when you're right and how much you lose when you're wrong.*
>
> —George Soros, hedge fund manager[1]

Life insurance companies like MetLife, Prudential, and State Farm have traditionally invested heavily in bonds. These investments have usually provided safety along with competitive yields. They also are more predictable compared to stocks.

But with interest rates at low levels, life insurance companies have been challenged in meeting their long-term obligations. Because of this, they have been investing more in alternative investments. These are assets that go beyond the typical stocks and bonds.

Life insurance companies have certainly not been the only ones that have been making this transition. Pension funds and university endowments have as well.

---

[1] www.investopedia.com/financial-edge/0511/the-top-17-investing-quotes-of-all-time.aspx

© Tom Taulli 2022
T. Taulli, *The Personal Finance Guide for Tech Professionals*,
https://doi.org/10.1007/978-1-4842-8242-7_3

While alternative investments have been mostly for institutions and wealthy investors, this trend is starting to change. The fact is that it is much easier for anyone to get exposure to this type of investment. This has been especially because of changes in regulations and the emergence of online platforms.

In the next five chapters, we'll take a look at the main categories of alternative investments: private equity, hedge funds, commodities/real estate/collectibles, angel investing, and crypto. As for this chapter, we'll cover the basics of alternative investments.

The Partnership Structure

Many alternative investments are part of a fund, and the structure is typically in the form of a partnership. This allows for more flexibility as well as tax advantages.

Keep in mind that a partnership is a pass-through structure. This means that profits and losses flow through it tax-free. Instead, the partnership will report any distributions to the IRS and other tax authorities by filing partnership returns. For those who invest in these funds, you will get a K-1 statement each year. This will report your gains and losses. You need to keep this in order to prepare your own tax return.

There are two types of partners. First, the general partner runs the partnership, and this is usually an investment firm. An example is Sequoia Capital, which Don Valentine founded in 1972. The firm currently has nearly 1,000 employees.

The leaders of Sequoia are the partners. They all have a "fiduciary duty" to their investors, which means acting in the best interests of the investors. As for the activities for a partner, they include

- Raise Capital: For a top firm like Sequoia, this is not particularly difficult. Because of its impressive long-term track record, there are many investors that want to invest. However, for a typical venture investment firm, the process is usually challenging and time-consuming. It could easily take a couple years. The fundraising will have a minimum threshold amount. Once this is met, the general managers can begin their investment activities. They can also continue to raise money for the fund.

- Investing: The partners will find deals and vet them. Usually, they will select a small number of them and negotiate the financings.

- Manage the Portfolio: The partners will track the performance of their investments. They will often help the companies, such as with recruiting employees, finding partners and referring potential customers. It's common for the partners to take some board seats for their investments.

- Follow-On Investments: The initial investment is usually not the last, at least when it comes to venture capital funds. The general partners will often participate on the next rounds of financing. This can help reduce the dilution of their stakes.

- Disclosures: Partners will provide periodic updates on the fund's progress, such as with quarterly letters and annual reports.

- Recruiting: Partners will spend considerable time building the team for their investment firm. Interestingly enough, founders and executives of portfolio companies may ultimately become partners.

- Skin-in-the-Game: Partners will usually be investors in the fund. This may account from 1% to 5% of the overall assets. This is to allow better alignment of interests between the partners and limited partners.

The general partner may have different vintages of funds. This means there are more than one version. These may be created every five to ten years. A general partner may also set up funds for different objectives. In the case of Sequoia, there is one for the United States, China, India, and Israel.

Next, an investment partnership will have limited partners, which commit money to the fund. They do not participate in the selection or management of the investments. This is why they are called "passive investors" and their investments are referred to as "blind pools."

Examples of limited partners include

- Corporate and Government Pensions: These organizations manage the money to finance the retirement of their workforces.

- Insurance companies: They generate substantial amounts of money from premiums from clients. This is known as the float. With it, insurance companies will allocate the money to long-term investments so as to pay off the long-term claims.

- Wealthy individuals: These are people who are classified as accredited investors (defined later in the chapter).

- Family Offices and Funds of Funds: These are money managers who invest the money of wealthy individuals or institutions.

- Sovereign Wealth Funds: These are state organizations that manage a government's excess reserves. Some of the largest funds include the Norway Government Pension Fund Global, China Investment Corporation, and the Kuwait Investment Authority.

- Private Foundations: These are organizations that are focused on charitable purposes. Some of the largest ones are the Melinda Gates Foundation, the Ford Foundation, and the Lilly Foundation.

Limited partners usually do not put up all the money upfront. Instead, they will allocate it based on the "cash calls" from the fund.

In terms of the fees for the general partner, here are the main ones:

- Management Fees: This is an annual fee that is based on the amount of assets in the fund. It often ranges from 1% to 3% and usually depends on the size of the fund. Basically, it is often higher for smaller funds. The fee is paid regardless of the performance. It is used to pay for the everyday costs, such as office rent, salaries, bonuses, software, subscriptions, and so on. Moreover, a fund contract may specify that the fee will be reduced over time as the investments are realized and distributions are made to the limited partners.

- Carried Interest: This is the incentive for the portfolio managers. The carried interest is a percentage of the profits of the fund. A common one is 20%.

- Other Fees: This includes income from consulting with portfolio companies, serving on the board of directors, or providing monitoring services. These fees may also involve equity compensation like stock options or restricted stock.

Let's take an example. Suppose you want to set up a venture capital firm. You have three other partners who will join the team. You will create a company called ABC Venture Partners and this will create a partnership for the first fund to invest in startups. The fund will be called ABC Venture Partners Fund I. For the next year, you raise $100 million from various endowments and insurance companies. These investors are the limited partners of the ABC Venture Partners Fund I.

There is a 2% management fee, which means you generate $2 million a year for the ABC Venture Partners. After this, you and your partners invest in eight startups. And this goes on for the next five years. In all, the ABC Venture Partners Fund I generated profits of $250 million and the carried interest is 20%. This means that 80% of the gains or $200 million go to the limited partners. As for the remaining profits, these go to the ABC Venture Capital Partners. The amount is $50 million. As you can see, it should be no surprise how venture capitalists can get rich! The carried interest on the gains on a large fund can definitely add up.

Here are some other concepts to understand about funds:

- Recycling: If there is a quick exit of a portfolio company – say within a couple years of the investment – then a portion of these proceeds may be put back into the fund. This can help increase the overall return.

- Claw back: When the fund closes and all the distributions are made to the limited partners, the general partners may have received excess amounts from the carried interest. A common reason for this is if there were losses generated in later years. When this happens, the general partners will need to return the excess amounts to the limited partners.

- Hurdle Rate: This is a minimum return that the limited partners will receive before the general partners get any carried interest. This is often set at 8%.

- Extensions: While the typical term of a fund is ten years, there may be a provision to extend this. A rule-of-thumb is to allow another two years or 10+2.

- Cash Calls: A general partner usually has contractual rights if a limited partner does not meet a cash call. Some of the actions include imposing higher interest or penalties, as well as forcing the sale of the interest.

Note   Limited partners are usually structured as tax-free organizations. This is why funds are often in the form of partnerships because they can distribute gains to the investors without triggering tax consequences.

The Pros and Cons of Alternative Investments

Let's first look at some of the main advantages of alternative investments:

- Lower Volatility: For the most part, the swings in asset values for alternative investments are generally muted. For example, based on the Goldman Sachs Alternative Investment Allocation Tool, putting 20% of a portfolio's assets into alternative assets means that there is lower volatility 100% of the time (this is based on returns from 1990 to 2018).[2] This assumes that the portfolio has 50% in stocks and 30% in bonds.

- Correlation: There is often low correlation between alternative investments and stocks and bonds. This can provide additional diversification for your portfolio. That is, if stocks and bonds fall, then alternative investments may see gains and vice versa. According to an iCapital Network survey of investment advisors, they consider diversification as one of the top reasons to invest in alternatives.[3]

- Talent: As noted, alternative investments can generate substantial compensation for portfolio managers. As a result, the industry attracts some of the world's best investors.

---

[2] www.gsam.com/content/gsam/us/en/advisors/resources/investment-ideas/liquid-alternatives/liquidaltstool.html

[3] www.icapitalnetwork.com/insights/research-practice-management/advisors-and-alternative-investments/

- Protections: Alternative investments often have more security for investors. The portfolio managers can negotiate directly to get better terms, such as with preferred stock. There may also be the grant of board seats. This type of control is more than about protections though. The investment firm will be in a position to guide the strategic position of the company. This may ultimately mean opting for certain long-term strategies.

- Taxes: You are usually a part-owner of the assets with alternative investments. And this can allow for attractive tax benefits. For example, it may mean getting to use depreciation or depletion deductions for real estate or oil/gas holdings. It is also possible to make investments in alternatives through retirement accounts like 401(k)s and IRAs. This can provide an additional layer of tax advantages.

- Income: Alternative investments can be structured to generate strong annual cash payments to investors, and they may be over 10%. This is especially the case with assets like real estate and pipelines.

- Flexibility: Traditional investments are focused mostly on making money when assets increase in value. But with alternatives, you can have portfolio managers use short selling or hedging. This can help soften the impact of bear markets. Note that there are some funds that are short only.

- Absolute Returns: Traditional investments are measured on relative returns. This means that the fund will compare itself to an index like the S&P 500.

If the index falls 10% but the fund is off by 8%, then this means that the relative performance was good. But of course, the portfolio would still be down. But with alternatives, the mandate is for absolute returns. This means that the portfolio managers will try to make positive returns regardless of the overall market moves.

Alternative investments definitely have their downsides too. The reality is that there are many that underperform traditional investments. Let's take a look at some of the key disadvantages:

- Fees: As seen earlier in this chapter, the fees can be substantial. This can make it tough for the limited partners to get strong returns.

- Access: You may be prohibited from investing in some types of funds that focus on alternatives. This could be that the fund is no longer available to outside investors, or they are very selective in who they allow to join. Some funds will simply want to only have institutional investors.

- Minimum investment: They can be high. Some may be $1 million or more.

- Transparency: The regulations for alternatives are not as stringent compared to publicly traded stocks and bonds. The reason is that the investors are considered to be "sophisticated" and are capable of doing their own due diligence. As a result, an alternative investment may not have extensive disclosures. In fact, another reason for this is that the fund wants to keep its investment strategies secret. In a way, an alternative investment can be like a "black box." Essentially, you are betting on the expertise and track record of the portfolio managers.

- Lockups or Gates: A fund may restrict you from selling any of your interest for a long period of time, say over a year. This is to allow the portfolio manager to invest for the long-term or have enough time to effectively sell illiquid assets.

- High Risk: The investments of a fund may be complex or illiquid. The portfolio manager may also take concentrated positions that can be risky.

- Drift: This is where the portfolio manager diverges from the investment focus. This may not necessarily be bad. But then again, it could mean that there are challenges with generating competitive returns.

With less transparency, there is the potential for more fraud. The biggest example of this was with Bernie Madoff. For decades, he masterminded a Ponzi scheme that amounted to nearly $65 billion. In 2009, he pleaded guilty to 11 felonies, such as for wire fraud, mail fraud, money laundering, and so on. The judge in the case sentenced Madoff to 150 years in prison. He would die in April 2021.

Of course, uncovering fraud is far from easy. But there are ways to do a background check. A simple approach is a Google search. You might find some stories about questionable actions or even convictions. Next, an investment advisor usually needs to file a Form ADV with the Securities and Exchange Commission or state regulators. It has three parts. But for the most part, they provide the following details of an investment advisor:

- The overall business

- Fees

- Assets under management

- Clients

- Conflicts of interest
- Disciplinary actions

You can look up a Form ADV at the Investment Adviser Public Disclosure (IAPD) website (`https://adviserinfo.sec.gov/`). Another useful resource is FINRA's BrokerCheck database, which provides background information on brokers and financial advisors (`https://brokercheck.finra.org/`).

J Curve

The J Curve is graph that shows the returns of a fund over time. As seen in Figure 3-1, it has a distinct J shape. The reason is based on the cash outflows and inflows over the life of a fund.

In the early years, there are mostly cash contributions from the limited partners. This means that the returns will increasingly go negative. True, there may be some early exits, but these will likely not have a big impact on the fund. If anything, bad investments tend to reveal themselves early in the investment period – which further depresses the returns.

But by year three to five, the returns should improve and when they hit the x axis, this will represent break-even for the fund. The top investments will start to show momentum. There will also be fewer outflows because much of the fund capital will have been invested.

The J Curve is remarkably consistent, even for the top funds. It highlights the importance of the long-term nature of these investments.

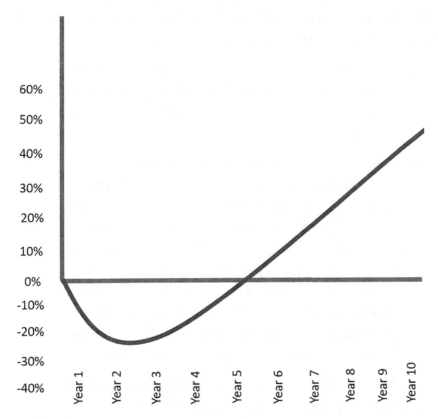

Figure 3-1. *This is the J Curve, which shows the returns of a fund over time*

Accredited Investors

For certain types of alternative investments, you will need to qualify as an accredited investor. Some of the common types include private securities – which have not been registered, say through an IPO – such as the sale of shares in startups (called a private placement) or interests in private equity funds or hedge funds.

The Securities and Exchange Commission sets forth the rules for being an accredited investor. They include the following:

- Annual income over $200,000 (if single) or $300,000 (if married and filing a joint return) for the past two years. You also need to indicate that you can maintain this for the current year.

- Net worth over $1 million, whether you are single or married and file a joint return. The net worth is the value of all your assets – which includes your vested employee stock options as well as property not held jointly with your spouse – minus your liabilities. This excludes the value of your principal residence. There is also a 60-day lookback rule. That is, if you take a loan against the value of your home during these last 60 days, you must include this in your liabilities for your net worth. This is a way to avoid inflating assets.

- You are a general partner, executive, or director for the company that is issuing the private securities.

- You are a registered broker or investment advisor.

- You have certain professional certifications or credentials, or you are a knowledgeable employee of a private fund.

The reason for the accredited investor rules is that there is less regulation for alternative investments. Thus, the SEC wants investors to be wealthier or have more investment experience to deal with the potential risks.

A trust is a common structure used to own assets. Thus it can qualify as an accredited investor. This is the case for both revocable and irrevocable trusts – if there is more than $5 million in assets, the trust was not formed for the sole purpose to invest in a fund, and the trustee is considered a sophisticated investor. A "sophisticated investor" is a person who has knowledge and experience in financial and business matters.

But there are other ways to qualify as an accredited investor:

- Revocable trust: Each grantor is an accredited investor and the tax benefits flow through directly to the grantors.

- Irrevocable trust: Each grantor is an accredited investor, the trust is a grantor trust, the grantor is the trustee, and the grantor is the sole source of the funding.

Access To Alternative Investors

For many alternative investments – like hedge funds, buyout funds, venture capital funds, and so on – individual investors usually work with financial advisors. Many of the large Wall Street firms have platforms that allow access. Table 3-1 shows some of the top companies.

Table 3-1. *Top Wealth Management Firms*

Firms
UBS Global Wealth Management
Credit Suisse
Morgan Stanley Wealth Management
Goldman Sachs
J.P. Morgan Private Bank
Charles Schwab
Bank of America GWIM
Citi Private Bank
Julius Baer
Northern Trust Wealth Management
BNY Mellon Wealth Management

Smaller wealth management firms may also provide access to alternative investments. They do this by using outsourced platforms like CAIS, Griffin Capital, and iCapital Network.

Regardless of the type of firm, there will be a minimum investment requirement. For the larger firms, this can be $1 million to $50 million. But the smaller wealth management firms may have thresholds at $25,000. Such an investment can then be integrated into an overall financial plan.

Note   According to the CEO of CAIS, independent financial advisors have anywhere from 1% to 2% of the portfolios invested in alternative investments.[4] But for large wealth management firms, the average is about 15% and institutions have allocations that range from 30% to 40%.

Conclusion

While stocks and bonds should be a part of any portfolio, there is also a need for alternative investments. They can help reduce volatility, provide diversification, and allow for the opportunity of higher returns.

But alternative investments can be complex and expensive. And yes, there have been notable cases of frauds. In other words, it's important to do your own due diligence before making an investment.

As for the next chapter, we'll look at hedge funds.

---

[4]www.wsj.com/articles/apollo-leads-225-million-investment-in-alternatives-platform-cais-11641898801?mod=lead_feature_below_a_pos1

CHAPTER 4

Hedge Funds

Benefiting from Sophisticated Investment Strategies

As for another profession...I suppose I'd manage a global-macro hedge fund. I love that kind of stuff. Weird, I know, but I find it fascinating.

—Nicholas Sparks, romance author[1]

In 1949, Alfred Winslow Jones created the first hedge fund. He was 48 years old and had no experience in the investing world. However, he was an avid reader of *Fortune* magazine, which inspired his thinking.

At the time, funds had mostly long-only positions, whether for stock or bond portfolios. But Winslow believed this strategy was tied too much to the direction of the market. His goal was to create a portfolio that was market neutral. In other words, his investments could post returns despite the swings in the market. He'd do this by having both long and short positions. This would essentially hedge the market. Because of this, he could focus on picking the right stocks.

---

[1] www.quotemaster.org/Hedge+Fund

© Tom Taulli 2022
T. Taulli, *The Personal Finance Guide for Tech Professionals*,
https://doi.org/10.1007/978-1-4842-8242-7_4

The performance of Winslow's fund was staggering. From 1956 to 1966, the return was 670%.[2] This compared to a 358% rise for the top mutual fund.

Fast forward to today: The hedge fund industry is enormous. There are over $4 trillion in assets under management, according to BarclaysHedge.[3]

What's more, hedge funds are more than just about market-neutral strategies. In fact, some of the approaches can be quite specialized and complex. So in this chapter, we'll look at the main types.

Sector Hedge Funds

Some hedge funds will focus primarily on certain market segments. This is often the case where the categories require deep expertise.

An example is biotech. Success is often about understanding cutting-edge medical applications. So, it is not surprising that many of the portfolio managers have medical degrees or PhDs.

But market-focused hedge funds can experience significant volatility. The fact is that sectors can quickly go out of favor.

This happened in 2021 with biotech hedge funds, as many of the top ones sustained major losses. They included Perceptive Advisors, which fell by 30% for the year, and OrbiMed Partners, which suffered a 40%+ drop.[4]

Then again, this came after two years of strong gains. These were primarily driven by the Covid-19 pandemic, which saw various innovations with vaccines.

---

[2] www.businessinsider.com/alfred-winslow-jones-started-the-first-hedge-fund-2016-8

[3] www.cnbc.com/2021/06/02/hedge-fund-assets-soar-to-record-high-amid-boom-in-trading-profits.html

[4] www.wsj.com/articles/hedge-funds-suffer-big-losses-on-biotech-rout-11638727155

Global Macro Hedge Funds

Global macro funds are seemingly limitless. A portfolio manager will look for investment opportunities across the world and use a myriad of investments, whether stocks, bonds, options, futures, swaps, and so on. For the most part, the trades are short term.

There are three main types of approaches to global macro hedge funds:

- Discretionary: The portfolio manager will use fundamental analysis when selecting investments. But this is usually about factoring in macroeconomic metrics, like inflation, interest rates, GDP rates, and currency movements.

- Commodity Trading Advisor (CTA): This is a person who trades commodities like gold, wheat, oil, and so on. This involves expertise with futures and options. A CTA gets certified with the National Futures Association (NFA), which allows for managing client funds. For the most part, the investment strategy focuses on technical analysis and computer-based algorithms.

- Systematic: This is where the manager uses a blend of fundamental and technical analysis in making investment decisions.

The emergence of global macro hedge funds came in the early 1970s. The main reason was the end of the Bretton Woods system, which provided for fixed exchange rates for currencies. But this was causing disruptions in the global economy, especially as inflation began to surge across the world. President Nixon took the United States off the international gold standard (this is where the dollar was backed by the convertibility into gold). Then in 1973, the US dollar and various other major currencies began to float against each other.

In the meantime, there was significant volatility in credit and stock markets. Then there was the oil crisis, as OPEC flexed its muscles.

Yet the environment provided ideal ways for global macro hedge funds to generate substantial profits. One of the best was George Soros' Quantum Fund, which he launched in 1970. He assembled a top-notch team that included investors like Jim Rogers and Stanley Druckenmiller.

Before making an investment decision, they would do considerable due diligence. A key part of this was looking at major global trends. For example, when the Yom Kippur War broke out between Israel and a coalition of Arab States, Soros, Rogers, and Druckenmiller realized that the US-built planes lagged. So they started buying up defense contractors, which were selling at low valuations. The premise was that there would be more investment in defense spending, which would ultimately happen in the early 1980s. There was also the benefit that contracts were long term and reliable – allowing for attractive profits.

Another major trade for the Quantum Fund was the shorting of the Nifty-Fifty stocks. In the early 1970s, the valuations hit stratospheric levels. But they could not be sustained, especially when the economy plunged into a recession in 1973 and 1974.

Next, there was a prescient short of gold, which reached a high $850 an ounce in 1980. Soros, Rogers, and Druckenmiller believed that the levels would not be sustainable, especially since inflation was likely to fall. By the early 1980s, gold was trading below $400 an ounce.

The bottom line: Quantum Fund pulled off an extraordinary run in the 1970s. During the decade, the gains were about 4,200%, versus a 47% increase in the S&P 500.[5]

---

[5]www.morningstar.in/posts/44056/makes-jim-rogers-great-investor.aspx

But this would not be the end of the success of the Quantum Fund.

Perhaps the most iconic trade occurred in 1992. Soros considered the British pound sterling to be overvalued, and he aggressively shorted the currency. The government tried to fight back, such as with aggressive purchases. But it was no use. The British sterling pound plunged, and Soros pocketed a $2 billion gain. In the media, Soros became known as the man who broke the Bank of England.[6]

However, as the Quantum fund grew much larger, it was getting difficult to post strong returns. As a result, Soros changed the mandate of the fund in 2000 and the focus became more conservative. In his last quarterly report to investors, he wrote: "An investment of $100,000 in the fund at its inception would be worth approximately $420 million today, provided that dividends could be reinvested at the net asset value of the fund (which was not the case)."[7]

This would actually represent a turning point for macro hedge funds. All in all, the returns would suffer during the next 20 years. Many of the top portfolio managers, like Paul Tudor Jones, Michael Platt, Louis Bacon, and Druckenmiller, would either reduce operations or even close their funds to new investors. It was common for them to just manage their own wealth, through a process of creating a family office.

In fact, after the financial crisis in 2008, the environment got particularly tough for macro hedge funds. This was due to the aggressive fiscal and monetary policies, which damped volatility.

Yet there are certainly standout macro hedge funds that have found ways to thrive – but they have had to be creative. Just look Jeffrey Talpins, who launched the Element Capital Management fund in 2005 with $250

---

[6] https://historyofyesterday.com/the-day-george-soros-broke-the-bank-of-england-to-make-1-1b-4834df0605d1

[7] https://money.cnn.com/2000/04/28/mutualfunds/soros/letter.htm

million in assets. Since then, the assets have ballooned to $16 billion.[8] Talpins relies mostly on sophisticated options strategies, which help to reduce risks as well as leverage gains.[9] The average annual returns since inception are over 18%.[10]

His team also does exhaustive research. An example was the analysis of the mRNA vaccines for the COVID-19 virus. Element Capital Management assessed that the efficacy would be much higher than expected. Because of this, the fund scored big returns on various investments, such as BioNTech.[11]

Note   In the 1920s and 1930s, John Maynard Keynes revolutionized macroeconomics. His theories showed the importance of fiscal policy in managing the economy. But he was also considered one of the first investors to use global macro strategies. From 1927 to 1946, Keynes ran the King's College endowment fund, which averaged annual returns of 9.1% versus a 1% decline in the British stock market.[12] When he died in 1946, his net worth was estimated at over $30 million.[13]

---

[8] www.elementcapital.com/jeffrey-talpins

[9] www.wsj.com/articles/jeffrey-talpins-is-the-hedge-fund-king-youve-never-heard-of-1543764284

[10] www.ft.com/content/157afec9-cb6f-469b-a5d0-c25b8fd6ac17

[11] www.ft.com/content/157afec9-cb6f-469b-a5d0-c25b8fd6ac17

[12] www.maynardkeynes.org/keynes-the-investor.html

[13] www.nytimes.com/2014/02/11/your-money/john-maynard-keyness-own-portfolio-not-too-dismal.html

Short Hedge Funds

Short hedge funds have a large portion of their portfolio in short positions. The category is fairly small, though. After all, short selling can be highly risky. A few bad investments can wreak havoc on a portfolio. Another problem is that bull markets tend to last much longer than bear markets. As a result, the performance for short hedge funds has underperformed from 2010 to 2021.

The "meme" bubble in early 2021 – which saw retail investors propel the stock prices of companies like GameStop and AMC – highlighted the dangers of short selling. Top hedge funds like Melvin Capital Management and D1 Capital Partners suffered huge losses.[14] To stave off liquidation, these firms had to raise capital. There was also the implementation of better risk controls.

Despite all this, short funds are still useful. Some investors will invest a small part of their portfolio in one to provide some downside protection.

A leading short only hedge fund is Kynikos (which is Greek for "cynic"). James Chanos founded this in 1985. Before this, he was a top Wall Street analyst and used deep fundamental analysis to uncover short sale opportunities, such as Baldwin-United (the company went bust in 1983).

Chanos' analysis also uses forensic accounting techniques. Essentially, this is about uncovering aggressive accounting practices that may be covering up poor performance of a company.

Look at what Chanos did with Enron. In 2000, he conducted a thorough deep dive on the company's financial statements. He found conflicts of interest, and questionable accounting approaches. He also saw that some of the company's financial results were not consistent with

---

[14] www.wsj.com/articles/gamestop-resurgence-reinforces-new-reality-for-hedge-funds-11614335400

what was happening in the rest of the market. For example, Enron showed growth with its broadband business even though the industry was quickly deteriorating. Interestingly enough, Chanos made money on shorting a variety of these stocks.

But there were other red flags. He saw that many Enron insiders were selling substantial amounts of stock. Then there was a quarterly earnings call, where Enron CEO Jeff Skilling called an analyst an "asshole." The analyst asked why the company did not provide a balance sheet.[15]

Chanos shorted Enron stock and by December 2001, the company filed for bankruptcy.

Quant Hedge Funds

A quant fund leverages sophisticated algorithms to make trades. These are based on processing huge amounts of data. The sources of this data often go beyond a company's financials. It may be about satellite information, weather patterns, scraping details from websites, social media sentiment, and so on.

Quant funds usually focus on short-term trading. In fact, this may mean holding onto a position for a few seconds. The idea is to find small discrepancies in the market and make tiny gains. But over time, these can definitely add up. But the trading can get costly as well. This is why a quant fund will try to find ways to reduce them. It also helps if there is a large amount of assets under management.

It's typical that the portfolio managers of quant funds will not have backgrounds in financial analysis. Instead, they will usually be computer scientists or data scientists. Some people will even have PhDs in areas that seemingly have nothing to do with investing, such as biochemistry or physics.

---

[15] www.wsj.com/articles/SB1004916006978550640

Take a look at D.E. Shaw Group, which Dr. David Shaw started in 1988. Before this, he was a professor of computer science at Columbia University where he researched parallel processing for supercomputers. This led to the creation of advanced systems to allow for searches of relational databases.

Dr. Shaw applied this experience in creating algorithms to detect inefficiencies in the financial markets. He also was a pioneer of high-speed trading. In the meantime, his fund would also pursue ventures, such as the creation of one of the first email hosting companies, Juno, during the mid-1990s.

Note   From 1990 to 1994, Jeff Bezos worked at D.E. Shaw Group and became a vice president. He led an effort to identify the most attractive opportunities in the nascent Internet market and his research led him to online book selling. But D.E. Shaw was not interested. So Bezos left the firm and went on to start Amazon.[16]

D.E. Shaw Group would have one of the best performances of any hedge fund.[17] By the end of 2021, the firm had about $60 billion under management.[18] Among its 1,300 employees, there were more than 80 PhDs, and over 500 engineers and developers.[19]

The algorithms for a quant fund are often referred to as black boxes. This means that they are extremely complicated and that the portfolio managers may not even understand why they work. Because of this, quant

---

[16] www.cnbc.com/2017/08/02/what-amazon-billionaire-jeff-bezos-was-doing-in-his-20s.html

[17] www.ft.com/content/90876f5c-6cf0-11ea-89df-41bea055720b

[18] www.deshaw.com/what-we-do/investment-approach

[19] www.ft.com/content/0364850c-3ebf-11e9-9bee-efab61506f44

funds will have some level of human intervention for trades. This is the case with D.E. Shaw Group. For example, in 2014, when Russia annexed Ukraine's Crimean landmass, the portfolio managers reduced investments on the Moscow exchange – even though the algorithms recommended otherwise.[20]

Another top quant hedge fund is Medallion, which is part Renaissance Technologies. Jim Simons started the firm in 1978. He was a PhD in mathematics and focused on geometry. In the 1960s, he actually worked at the National Security Agency to break Russian codes while he taught at MIT and Harvard.

As for his hedge fund, Simons used machine learning and artificial intelligence to build his models. He realized that computers could recognize patterns that humans could not – and in real time. Simons also understood the power of data. He would invest heavily in datasets, with some going back to the 1700s.[21]

And yes, the strategy worked extremely well. From 1998 to 2019, the Medallion Fund averaged returns of 66% per year or 39% after subtracting the fees.[22]

The IT platform of the company is enormous. There are 35,000 processors that apply algorithms across 30 trillion bytes of data. The software has over ten million lines of code.[23]

---

[20] www.ft.com/content/0364850c-3ebf-11e9-9bee-efab61506f44

[21] www.cnbc.com/2019/11/05/how-jim-simons-founder-of-renaissance-technologies-beats-the-market.html

[22] www.cnbc.com/2019/11/05/how-jim-simons-founder-of-renaissance-technologies-beats-the-market.html

[23] www.wsj.com/articles/renaissance-s-10-billion-medallion-fund-gains-24-year-to-datein-tumultuous-market-11587152401

Now there are certain quant funds that can badly misjudge the markets. In some cases, the results can be disastrous, especially when there are heavy amounts of borrowed capital.

An example of this was Long-Term Capital Management (LTCM), whose motto was "The Financial Technology Company." In 1993, John Meriwether founded the firm and brought on Nobel winners, Myron Scholes and Robert C. Merton, as advisors. The focus was on identifying small anomalies in prices among bonds. And the strategy worked extremely well. The LTCM fund was racking up 40%+ returns.

But by 1997, it was getting harder to find investment opportunities. So LTCM looked beyond bonds and started to make bets on mergers. There was also an aggressive move into fixed-income securities in emerging markets. But perhaps the most dangerous move was to significantly increase the borrowing of the fund, which got to $50 in debt for each dollar in equity.[24]

By 1998, the LTCM fund was in serious trouble. The global markets were getting volatile. Next, there was the default of Russian government bonds, which LTCM's algorithms did not consider a possibility.

During late summer, LTCM was on the verge of collapse. Officials at the Federal Reserve were worried that this could be a disaster for the global financial system. To avert this, they assembled a group of 14 banks and Wall Street firms to bailout LTCM for $3.625 billion.

Hybrid Hedge Funds

Generally, hedge funds invest in publicly traded securities. The main reason is that they are generally liquid, which makes it easier to handle large transactions without suffering big drops in price.

---

[24] www.wsj.com/articles/SB911168945488412500

But during the past decade, some hedge funds have been investing more in private companies. Often these are high-tech startups that are backed by venture capitalists. Since these companies have usually taken longer to come public, hedge funds have been a source of capital. Some of the largest hybrid hedge funds include D1 Capital Partners, Whale Rock Capital Management, Viking Global Investors, and Tiger Global Management.

With the strong growth in the technology sector, the hybrid funds have been able to juice their gains. From 2010 to 2020, the average returns for venture investments were 14.2%, which was twice as much for the typical hedge fund.[25]

No doubt, there is an opportunity to get returns that can be a game-changer for a fund. An example is Maverick Capital's $20 million investment in Coupang, which is a top ecommerce operator in South Korea. By the time of the IPO in 2021, the shares fetched a valuation of $3.9 billion.[26]

Hybrid funds, though, have limits on the percentage of their portfolio that can be allocated to private investments (say 15% to 25%). They may also have different share classes for its limited partners. This allows them to have different levels of exposure. However, by 2022, these types of funds came under pressure because of the bear market in tech stocks.

---

[25] www.wsj.com/articles/as-hedge-funds-endure-rocky-year-private-company-bets-ease-the-pain-11634981400

[26] www.wsj.com/articles/hedge-funds-increase-bets-on-private-companies-11621416604

Alternative Credit Hedge Funds

Alternative credit hedge funds involve a myriad of strategies. They may include funds making direct loans to companies, buying distressed debt, arranging financing for buyouts, providing capital for real estate projects and so on.

With interest rates at low levels, there has been much interest in alternative credit hedge funds because the returns tend to be higher. From 2010 to 2021, the assets under management for this category have gone from $341 billion to $975 billion.[27]

The 2008 financial crisis has been another catalyst for alternative credit hedge funds. The reason is that federal regulations made it difficult for traditional banks and Wall Street firms to facilitate the financings. Hedge funds have filled the void.

Alternative credit usually is in maturities of one to ten years and the annual returns have ranged from 5% to 10% per year. To help achieve these levels, a fund will borrow money.[28]

The future looks promising for alternative credit hedge funds. According to a survey – which involved firms like Vanguard, Goldman Sachs, and BlackRock – the returns are expected to average 7.7% from 2020 to 2030.[29] This compares to only 2.70% for US corporate bonds.

---

[27] www.wsj.com/articles/ares-raises-8-billion-fund-in-private-credit-arms-race-11639391408

[28] www.wsj.com/articles/ares-raises-8-billion-fund-in-private-credit-arms-race-11639391408

[29] www.wsj.com/articles/ares-raises-8-billion-fund-in-private-credit-arms-race-11639391408

A key advantage for alternative credit hedge funds is that they can negotiate strong protections. For example, in a real estate project, this could mean getting equity. Or there may be debt structures that have higher priorities or liens on certain assets.

Access to alternative credit hedge funds has been mostly for institutions. But this is starting to change. Blackstone has created platforms BREIT (https://www.breit.com/) and BCRED (https://www.bcred.com/) that allow accredited investors to participate.

Arbitrage Hedge Funds

Arbitrage is a popular strategy for hedge funds. It is about capitalizing on mispricing of the same or similar assets in different markets. To understand this, let's take an example. Suppose XYZ Corp. is traded on the NYSE and the Tokyo exchange. But there is a difference in the prices. On the NYSE, the shares are trading at $100 whereas they are $100.50 on the Tokyo exchange.

A hedge fund can use an arbitrage strategy to make a profit on this trade. This means buying the shares at $100 on the NYSE and shorting the same number at $100.50 on the Tokyo exchange. Eventually, the spread will disappear, and the investor will keep the difference.

Granted, this is a simple example. Keep in mind that arbitrage strategies can get extremely complicated, involving sophisticated computer programs. The mispricing may only last a few seconds.

An advantage of arbitrage is the low risk. This is especially the case when the asset is the same, as in our XYZ Corp example. However, the risk levels are higher when the trade involves different securities. This is when the focus is on merger opportunities.

Let's take an example. ABC Corp., which is trading at $50, agrees to pay $25 a share for Cool Corp. The shares of Cool Corp. surge from $15 to $24.

But why not to $25? The reason is that an acquisition can take at least a few months to close. In the meantime, there is risk that the deal may fail. The spread between $24 and $25 a share is Wall Street's way of estimating this possibility.

But if an arbitrage fund believes the deal will happen, it will buy the shares of Cool Corp. and wait to get paid the $25. However, if this scenario does not play out, the stock price is likely to plunge. The losses are often magnified since a merger arbitrage fund will often use borrowed money for the position.

Now there are other types of arbitrage strategies. Here's a look:

- Convertible Arbitrage: If there is a mispricing, the hedge fund will take a long position in the convertible bond and short the stock. Although, the strategy can prove risky during highly volatile markets. This happened during the financial crisis in 2008, in which convertible arbitrage funds lost an average of 33.7%.[30]

- Relative Value Arbitrage or Pairs Trading: This is where there are mispricings between investments that have correlation with each other. This could, for example, be between stocks and options.

Hedge Fund ETFs

There are a variety of ETFs that use hedge fund strategies. They are often based on indexes. But some involve portfolio managers as well that actively trade the portfolio. All in all, the ETFs can provide an easy and low-cost way to get some exposure to hedge funds.

---

[30] www.ft.com/content/33f1d1f7-745e-4fd2-ae25-a34e0b035f94

Here's a look:

- ProShares Hedge Replication ETF (HDG): While the fund does not invest in hedge funds, it is based on the Merrill Lynch Factor Model, which reflects the performance of over 2,000 funds.[31] This involves using short and long positions across the S&P 500, the MSCI EAFE US Dollar Net Total Return Index, the MSCI Emerging Markets US Dollar Net Total Return Index, the Russell 2000 Total Return Index, the three-month US Treasury bills, and the ProShares UltraShort Euro ETF.

- IQ Merger Arbitrage ETF (MNA): This is based on the IQ Merger Arbitrage Index.[32] It will purchase stocks where there have been public announcements of a takeover or merger. The investments are only on larger stock markets and the positions are liquidated when a deal is closed. The fund will also have some short positions to hedge the portfolio.

- iShares Convertible Bond ETF (ICVT): This tracks the Bloomberg Barclays US Convertible Cash Pay Bond > $250MM Index.[33] It has convertible bonds that pay only cash, and the securities are not required to be converted.

---

[31] www.proshares.com/our-etfs/strategic/hdg

[32] www.newyorklifeinvestments.com/etf/iq-merger-arbitrage-etf-mna?ticker=MNA

[33] www.ishares.com/us/products/272819/ishares-convertible-bond-etf

- IQ Hedge Multi-Strategy Tracker ETF (QAI): This is based on an index that attempts to replicate a variety of hedge fund strategies like long/short equity, global macro, market neutral, and fixed-income arbitrage.[34] This is done by investing in a variety of ETFs as well as futures contracts and swaps.

- Invesco S&P 500 Low Volatility ETF (SPLV): A minimum of 90% of the assets are invested in 100 of the securities with the lowest volatility – for the past 12 months – of the S&P 500.[35] This often means the companies are in stable industries like utilities or consumer staples. The strategy helps to reduce the potential downside of the fund. Although, when the markets are in extreme conditions, the losses can still be considerable – but usually not as bad as the overall market.

- First Trust Long/Short Equity ETF (FTLS): The fund invests in long and short positions of stocks and ETFs in the United States and in foreign markets.[36] The investment selection is based on a variety of approaches like fundamental analysis, technical analysis, and statistical attributes. For the most part, 80% to 100% of the positions will be long and 0% to 50% will be short.

---

[34] www.newyorklifeinvestments.com/etf/iq-hedge-multi-strategy-tracker-etf-qai

[35] www.invesco.com/us/financial-products/etfs/product-detail?audienceType=investors&productId=splv

[36] www.ftportfolios.com/retail/etf/etfsummary.aspx?Ticker=FTLS

- AdvisorShares Active Bear ETF (HDGE): This ETF invests at least 80% of its assets in short positions in stocks.[37] The portfolio manager does extensive fundamental analysis of its investments, such as to identify low earnings quality or aggressive accounting. The HDGE ETF can be used as part of a long/short strategy when it is paired with a long-index ETF, such as one based on the S&P 500.

- ProShares Short S&P 500 ETF (SH): These are inverse index funds. So if the S&P 500 falls by 1%, then this ETF will increase by 1% and vice versa.[38] This fund is a way to provide a hedge against any potential market declines.

- Cambria Tail Risk ETF (TAIL): This fund helps to reduce the downside risk of a portfolio. This is done by purchasing put options that are out of the money (this means that there is no intrinsic value). As a result, if there is a major downward move in the markets, this fund should do quite well.[39]

---

[37] advisorshares.com/etfs/hdge/

[38] www.proshares.com/our-etfs/leveraged-and-inverse/sh

[39] https://cambriafunds.com/tail

Note   Sculptor Capital Management (NYSE:SCU) is the only publicly traded hedge fund in the United States. In has portfolios for multi-strategy, credit, and real estate. The assets under management are more than $38 billion.[40]

Multi-strategy Hedge Funds

As the name implies, a multi-strategy hedge fund will use various investment approaches. The purpose is to benefit from the diversification of uncorrelated asset classes. This provides for lower volatility over the long-term.

The organization of a multi-strategy hedge fund can lead to complications. After all, there is a main portfolio manager for each fund, and they will be allocated a certain amount of capital. No doubt, this can lead to infighting. In some cases, a portfolio manager will even leave.

The organization structure can also get difficult with managing risk. This is why multi-strategy hedge funds are usually large organizations that have strong management systems.

Another issue of a multi-strategy hedge fund is the compensation since there are numerous portfolio managers. To deal with this, a fund will often use "pass-through" fees, which allow for expenses for such things as bonuses, deferred compensation, travel, and so on. Yet these will increase the overall fees for the funds. Over the years, more and more investors have been pushing back on this.

---

[40]`www.sculptor.com/our-business`

One of the largest multi-strategy funds is DE Shaw, which uses different strategies that focus on absolute returns. Since 2001, it has posted a net average annual gains of 11.78% and there was only one losing year.[41]

Another top multi-strategy hedge fund is Citadel's Wellington fund. Its strategies are global macro, credit, quantitative, global fixed income, commodities, and equities.[42] Besides a strong team of portfolio managers, Citadel also has the benefit of a sophisticated risk management system.[43]

Ken Griffin, the CEO and founder of Citadel, has said: "Business is business. I don't manufacture cars, but we do manufacture money."[44]

Now, a multi-strategy fund is often confused with a fund of funds (FOF) hedge fund. But there are clear differences. An FOF has a portfolio manager that will invest in various other hedge funds. In other words, the investors have the opportunity to get wide exposure to high-quality funds. The FOF portfolio manager will handle the due diligence, monitor the investments, and help with the asset allocation.

True, this means that there will be two layers of fees: one for the FOF portfolio manager and another for the hedge funds. But for investors that do not have the resources to invest in these types of services, an FOF can be a good option.

---

[41] www.hedgeweek.com/2021/01/12/294291/de-shaw-delivers-strong-returns-2020

[42] www.cnbc.com/2021/10/04/ken-griffins-citadel-flagship-hedge-fund-returns-8percent-in-september-during-market-sell-off.html

[43] www.ft.com/content/33c190fe-dfb1-43c2-82eb-5396a986f342

[44] www.wsj.com/articles/citadels-ken-griffin-leaves-2008-tumble-far-behind-1438655887

Specialized Hedge Funds

Some hedge funds do not fit within the typical categories. They will instead specialize in a niche area of investment, which often provide interesting investment opportunities.

Here's a look at some of them:

- Shipping: The hedge fund will purchase large container ships, which can generate substantial fees through long-term contracts. An example is Mangrove Partners, which has $1.3 billion in assets. The fund made its purchases of container ships during a period when the industry was struggling (the founder, Nathaniel August, named the ships after the names of top players on the New England Patriots). Then, when the Covid-19 pandemic hit, there were major issues with the global supply chain, and this resulted in much higher profits. For 2021, the Mangrove fund returned a hefty 71%.[45]

- Litigation: Yes, a hedge fund will purchase the rights to legal cases. It could be for a major class action suit or even a mega divorce. The hedge fund will fund the legal services and then get a piece of the judgement. It's a risky type of investment, as juries can be unpredictable. This is why some of the hedge funds will finance a variety of different cases. The litigation finance industry was $39 billion – on a global basis – as of 2019.[46] Some of the funds that are major players in the market include Elliot Management and DE Shaw Group.

---

[45] www.wsj.com/articles/supply-chain-snarls-deliver-windfalls-to-wall-street-11637231401

[46] www.insurancejournal.com/news/national/2021/11/16/642401.htm

- Music Rights: A musician's copyrights can be quite valuable. For example, in 2021, investment firm KKR and BMG spent a minimum of $1 billion for the music of ZZ Top, Stevie Wonder, Adele, and Beyoncé.[47] These rights generate strong income and have benefited from the growth in streaming. But there is also an opportunity for professional money managers to find ways to improve the returns, such as with using the music for television commercials and movies.

Activist Hedge Funds

Some hedge funds will take aggressive actions to agitate for change. These are known as activist funds. They will usually take large positions in company's stock and then write a letter to the board of directors. The letter will indicate how management has underperformed and there will be certain actions to take, such as to exit a business, cut costs, or go private. Some of the well-known activist hedge funds include Starboard Value, ValueAct Capital, and Elliott Management.

But the investments are not necessarily with stocks either. Some activist hedge funds will wage battles against governments. And they often go to extraordinary lengths with their investments. Look at Paul Singer, who is the founder of Elliott Management. During the 1980s, he made strong returns investing in distressed corporate debt. He then focused on buying defaulted government debt or sovereign debt. In the early 2000s, he purchased Argentinian bonds and sued for repayment. But the government balked. Undeterred, Singer continued his aggressive legal

---

[47] www.wsj.com/articles/kkr-and-bmg-buy-into-zz-tops-music-11640088004?mod=hp_lista_pos3

fight. In 2012, he attempted to seize an Argentine Navy vessel, which was docked at the Port of Tema, in Ghana. But the cadets on board threatened to fight back. In the meantime, the legal battle remained, and Singer would ultimately win his case in 2016. His judgment was for $2.4 billion or a 1,270% return.[48]

The Big Trade

In 2006, hedge fund manager John Paulson saw that the home mortgage market was quickly becoming a bubble. The underwriting standards were quite lax, and the losses were starting to pile up.

Paulson set out to bet his fund on shorting the market. But this was not easy. So he looked at a niche in the markets called credit-default swaps, which were like options to bet against mortgage portfolios.

Of course, Paulson's trade wound up being spot on – and one of the most successful ever. From 2007 and 2008, he generated profits of about $20 billion and his own share was $4 billion.[49]

However, this would turn out to be the end of Paulson's successful big trades. Given the enormous size of his fund – the peak was $38 billion in 2011 – it was tough to find new opportunities. He would eventually convert it into a family office and return the investor capital.

Thus, when it comes to hedge funds, it's important to be realistic. Red-hot investors often go cold – and this can happen quickly. Instead, the focus should be on those who have shown consistent long-term results.

---

[48] www.newyorker.com/magazine/2018/08/27/paul-singer-doomsday-investor
[49] www.wsj.com/articles/hedge-fund-star-john-paulson-calls-it-quits-11593637778

Conclusion

From 2010 to 2020, the overall performance of the typical hedge fund has lagged the markets. A big reason for this is the lower volatility because of the Federal Reserve's low interest rate policy.

But this may not last. The next decade could easily see more volatility, and this could mean that hedge funds will benefit.

One of the key benefits is the ability to short the markets. This can help to soften the downturns. But hedge funds also can invest across global markets, in any type of investment vehicle, and employ sophisticated strategies, such as by using AI and machine learning.

On the other hand, there needs to be due diligence when investing in hedge funds. This is why fund-of-funds managers are popular. They can help put a plan in place.

Or, if you are not a wealthy investor, you can get exposure to hedge fund strategies via ETFs.

In the next chapter, we'll take a look at private equity, which includes such things as buyouts, venture capital, and angel investing.

CHAPTER 5

Private Equity

Buyouts, Venture Capital, and Angel Investing

The venture capital business is a 100% game of outliers. It's extreme exceptions.

—Marc Andreessen, Internet pioneer and VC[1]

During the dotcom bust, Ben Chestnut, Dan Kurzius, and Mark Armstrong founded a web design agency. They not only built sites for clients but also for themselves. One was for e-greetings. But unfortunately, it did not get much interest from users. Yet there was a silver lining: It had a popular character that was a chimp. The founders would use this for another site, which was Mailchimp.

But it was mostly a side project. Yet by 2007, Mailchimp continued to show progress and the founders would focus on this full time.

It was certainly a smart move. By leveraging the freemium model, Mailchimp became a leading email marketing platform.

---

[1] https://medium.com/how-to-start-a-startup/17-quotes-from-marc-andreessen-ron-conway-on-how-to-raise-money-d0b710f115f1

© Tom Taulli 2022
T. Taulli, *The Personal Finance Guide for Tech Professionals,*
https://doi.org/10.1007/978-1-4842-8242-7_5

By 2021, it had a global base of 13 million users and 800,000 paid customers. The revenues reached $800 million. At the time, the founders decided to sell the company to Intuit for a whopping $12 billion.[2]

Something else to consider: Mailchimp did not raise any outside institutional capital during its history. The business was essentially a classic bootstrap.

Note that this is extremely rare in the startup world. The fact is that companies usually need lots of capital to build the product, find customers, and develop the infrastructure.

The capital usually does not come from banks. Instead, the providers are private equity firms, and the main ones include buyout, growth, and venture capital firms. There are also angel investors and crowdfunding for early-stage ventures.

Besides providing capital, private equity has generally been a good source of returns for investors. So, in this chapter, we'll take a closer look at this asset class.

Buyout Funds

Buyouts are not new. The origins go back to the 1800s with the emergence of the Industrial Revolution. Some of the notable dealmakers included Jay Gould and JP Morgan.

But the modern approach to buyouts came in the 1970s. This is when the first fund came about. The partners included Wall Street veterans Jerome Kohlberg, Henry Kravis, and George Roberts, who started KKR, and the first fund was set at $25 million. Their strategy for buyouts has actually remained quite similar to the deals structured today.

---

[2]www.forbes.com/sites/tomtaulli/2021/09/25/12-billion-for-mailchimp-lessons-for-entrepreneurs/?sh=6ab3864f29e5

For example, suppose ABC Corp. is publicly traded but the stock price has lagged. The CEO of the firm contacts KKR to take the company private. With this, the firm will buy all the shares and ABC Corp. will return to being a privately held company.

Why do this? This can help management focus more on long-term initiatives, not the quarterly expectations of Wall Street. Another reason is that the company's stock is usually undervalued.

Being private will not usually be the end game. After all, KKR's investors want to make money. This comes by taking the company public again or selling it to another firm.

A key to this is for KKR to implement restructuring plans to improve operations and margins. This could mean layoffs and sell-offs of non-core divisions. There may also be a focus on acquisitions to bolster the business. Since a private equity firm will have majority control, it is much easier to take these types of actions.

Another important aspect of a buyout is to provide incentives for management to focus on improving shareholder value. This involves allocating large equity stakes for them. In other words, the management team could become wealthy if the performance of the company is strong.

In terms of the valuations on buyout deals, they are generally based on a multiple of EBITDA. This is a company's earnings before interest, taxes, depreciation, and amortization. For the most part, it is a way to measure the underlying cash flow of a company.

OK then, to continue with our example, let's suppose ABC Corp. and KKR agree to a deal for $1 billion. The company has EBITDA of $200 million.

However, KKR will not put up all the money. Instead, it will write a check for, say, $100 million of the equity and borrow the rest (this is why a buyout is often called a leveraged buyout or LBO).

The valuation of the deal is actually $1.9 billion, which is known as the enterprise value. This is the equity value of $1 billion plus the debt of $900 million. As for the EBITDA multiple, it is the enterprise value divided by the EBITDA or 9.5X.

In terms of the funding for the deal, part of it will come from banks, which will provide secured loans. Then there will be another level of debt that is riskier but has higher returns. This is often high yield or junk bonds. During the 1970s and 1980s, the biggest player in this market was Mike Milken.

The leveraged structure is a way to juice up the return. For example, suppose ABC Corp. comes public again four years later and the valuation is $2 billion, or $1.1 billion after netting out the debt. This would mean that the return on the $100 million for KKR would be 11X or $1.1 billion divided by $100 million.

In light of these returns, buyout funds became one of the hottest investments during the 1980s. But this also attracted lots of other competitors. As valuations and debt levels got higher, it became more difficult to make money on the deals.

The peak in the buyout market came in 1988. This is when KKR sought a mega deal for RJR Nabisco, which erupted into a bidding war. But the firm would win the deal for a hefty $25 billion (this would stand as the biggest buyout until the $33 billion transaction for HCA in 2006).

Note   In 1989, *Wall Street Journal* reporters Bryan Burrough and John Helyar published *Barbarians at the Gate*, which chronicled the drama-filled story of the RJR Nabisco buyout. The book has since become a classic in the business world. It would also be made into an HBO film in 1993.

However, the deal would turn out to be one of the worst for KKR. Some of the reasons were the seizing of the junk bond market (which resulted in higher interest costs), discounting on cigarettes from rival Philip Morris, and difficulties with selling off assets.

As a result, KKR's 1987 vintage fund – which included the RJR deal – would be the lowest performer. Its average annual return was 12% versus 26% for all the rest. If the RJR deal had not been completed, the fund would have had a gain of 25.2%.[3]

The good news is that private equity firms learned from this experience. Not only would they be more disciplined with valuations, but also be mindful with debt structures, and projections. For the most part, the buyout market has remained a strong source of competitive returns.

Keep in mind that buyout funds tend to focus on traditional businesses like consumer goods, financial services, energy, healthcare, and so on. After all, to pay for the debt, there needs to be stable cash flows.

But during the past decade, buyout funds have been getting more aggressive with technology deals. The focus has generally been on companies with durable revenue streams and large customer bases. For example, in 2021, KKR and Global Infrastructure Partners agreed to pay close to $12 billion for CyrusOne, which operates data centers. Then there was $12 billion buyout of McAfee, a top developer of security software. The buyers included Advent International and Permira.[4]

Besides going private transactions, there are other transactions available. They include the following:

- Private Company Deals: A private equity firm may buy a privately held company. This is often an operation that is family owned. The private equity firm may ultimately take the company public or sell it to another company.

- Secondary Transaction: This is when a private equity firm will buy a company from another fund.

---

[3] www.privateequityinternational.com/special-reportbrrjr-nabisco-20th-anniversary/

[4] www.wsj.com/articles/private-equity-backs-record-volume-of-tech-deals-11641207603?mod=lead_feature_below_a_pos1

- Division: This is where a private equity firm will buy a subsidiary of a larger company. These are common transactions because the business is often neglected. This means that a private equity firm has an opportunity to improve the operations of the division, which should lead to higher returns.

- Privatization: This is common in countries like China that have many state-owned businesses. One way to privatize them is to sell the operations to private equity funds.

Venture Capital Funds

In the summer of 2012, data warehousing veterans Benoit Dageville, Thierry Cruanes, and Marcin Żukowski founded Snowflake. Their vision was to create a native-cloud database platform.

The founders got a $5 million Series A round of financing from Sutter Hill, a top venture capital firm in Silicon Valley. They initially used the VC's offices and one of the partners of the VC fund became the temporary CEO.

It took several years to build the product. But once it was launched, it saw strong growth.

In September 2020, Snowflake pulled off its IPO and raised $3.4 billion, making it the largest software offering ever.[5] Investors in the IPO included Salesforce.com and Warren Buffett's Berkshire Hathaway.

As for Sutter Hill, the firm snagged one of the biggest hauls for VCs. The firm had invested roughly $190 million and generated a profit of $12 billion.[6]

---

[5] www.cnn.com/2020/09/16/investing/snowflake-ipo/index.html
[6] www.wsj.com/articles/venture-firms-bask-in-a-surge-of-blockbuster-profits-11619608939

Consider that this was not necessarily a rare event. Take a look at Sequoia. It invested a total of $235 million in Airbnb and the shares soared to $14 billion when the company came public in December 2020. Then the firm profited $8.4 billion on its $240 million investment in DoorDash.

Amazing, right? Definitely. But when it comes to investing, whenever there are staggering returns, there are substantial risks. This is no different with VCs. Even the elite firms have made terrible investments.

But this is part of the strategy, actually. The fact is that startups often fail. A general rule of thumb is that half of the portfolio of a VC will have deals that decline in value or go to zero. Then there will be 20% to 30% that will be singles or doubles. And finally, there will be a handful of deals that have standout returns. Basically, the overall performance really hinges on just a few transactions. If they are not good enough, then the VC fund will probably greatly underperform the S&P 500.

Burgiss Group LLC conducted a study on the performance of venture capital funds from 2010 to 2015 and the average return was close to 16%.[7] However, the top 5% of the funds posted returns of more than 42%.

Note   Because of the need for huge returns, a VC fund does not conform to the typical bell curve. Rather, it is more skewed at the tails. This is known as the power law curve.

Unlike buyout funds, VCs will take minority positions in their investments, say 10% to 20% of the equity. This is to provide significant incentives for the team to achieve stretch goals.

---

[7]www.wsj.com/articles/venture-firms-bask-in-a-surge-of-blockbuster-profits-11619608939

There will also likely be several rounds of financing for these startups. They will be burning money so as to hire employees, expand the products, and spend money on sales and marketing. There will also be low levels of revenues, at least in the early years. Successful VC-backed companies usually raise hundreds of millions in capital before they go public.

Venture capitalists will get preferred stock. This will mean that they will get priority whenever there is a liquidity event, such as a buyout, IPO, or even bankruptcy. This is expressed in a liquidation preference.

For example, suppose Sequoia invests $50 million in ABC Corp. For this, they receive preferred shares that have a 1X liquidation preference. Thus, if there is a buyout, Sequoia will get its $50 million back before any other investors. Then the amounts above this will be allocated based on the ownership positions. In some cases, a VC can negotiate 2X or even 3X liquidation preferences. Although, these are fairly rare.

Note   Each VC investment is called a series round. So the first one is the Series A round and the next is the Series B round, and so on. A round will also generally have more than one investor (this is known as a "club deal") so as to spread the risk. But there are one or two VCs that will lead the deal. They will be in charge of negotiation and have the largest equity stakes.

A VC will negotiate other protections for their investments, including:

- Anti-Dilution Clauses: This is for when the next round of funding for a startup is at a lower valuation. To make up for the dilution, the VC will get extra shares. But this will severely cut into the ownership positions of the founders, employees, and other investors.

- Representation: It's common for VCs to get board seats. This provides more control over the strategic direction of the company. However, in some cases, a VC will have observer rights on the board. This allows them to attend meetings, but not have a vote.

- Veto Rights: This allows the VCs the ability to deny certain actions. Common ones are the issuance of new shares, amendments to the certificate of incorporation, the hiring of senior executives and executives.

- Preemptive Rights: This gives the VC a right-of-first-refusal if a shareholder wants to sell their holdings. This can prevent the shares from being transferred to a competitor. Interestingly enough, this happened in 2004 when a Craigslist shareholder sold a 28.4% stake to rival eBay.[8]

It's true that some VCs will invest at the founding of a company. But typically, a firm wants to see some proof-of-concept, such as with a prototype or initial traction with customers.

No doubt, the valuation of these deals can be extremely difficult. Given that there may be minimal revenues, VCs will need to look at alternative approaches. One is to use the valuations in comparable deals.

Regardless, VCs will want to focus on those startups that have the potential for huge returns. This means that the total addressable market (TAM) must be large, say over $1 billion.

Another important factor that VCs look for is that the product or service solves a tough problem – and is done much better than the alternatives. If this is not the case, the startup will likely not succeed.

---

[8] www.theguardian.com/technology/2008/apr/24/ebay.internet

Note   Losses for a VC portfolio are normal. But the biggest risk for a firm is missing out on a mega deal. This happens to even the best firms. Consider Bessemer Venture Partners. The firm actually published an anti-portfolio of missed deals. Some include Airbnb, Coinbase, Apple, Google, Facebook, Zoom, PayPal, Intel, and eBay. Despite this, Bessemer Venture Partners still has a strong long-term record for its investors

---

Some VC funds will focus on growth equity opportunities. This means that the companies are in later stages of development. For example, the revenues may be in excess of $100 million. Often these deals are known as unicorns because the valuations are over $1 billion. Many of these companies will either attempt to go public soon or sell to a larger company.

Rethinking the Venture Capital Model

VCs are always on the hunt for finding disruptive companies. These types of startups can achieve huge returns, as seen with companies like Uber and Airbnb.

But the irony is that the venture capital industry has seen little change since the early days of the 1970s. According to a blog post from Sequoia partner Roelof Botha: "As chips shrank and software flew to the cloud, venture capital kept operating on the business equivalent of floppy disks."[9]

But some of the leading firms, like Sequoia and Andressen Horowitz, are rethinking their approaches. A big reason for this is the increased

---

[9] https://medium.com/sequoia-capital/the-sequoia-fund-patient-capital-for-building-enduring-companies-9ed7bcd6c7da

competition. VC firms have to contend with family offices and even institutions that make direct investments into private companies.

To evolve, more VCs have elected to become Registered Investment Advisors, which requires getting registered with the Securities and Exchange Commission. While this is expensive and results in more regulation, the RIA allows much more flexibility. A firm can own larger amounts of publicly traded shares, but also digital assets like crypto currencies and NFTs (non-fungible tokens).

Next, VCs have been getting more innovative in how they source new deals and help entrepreneurs. Some of the initiatives include hiring scouts to find interesting startups and creating educational programs.

Another change for VCs is to abandon the 10-year fund cycle. A reason for this is that – even after a company goes public – they can continue to generate significant returns. This has certainly been the case with companies like Google, Apple, Facebook, Square, and so on.

For Sequoia, it has created an evergreen fund, called the Sequoia Capital Fund. There is no time limit to it. Here's how Botha explains it:

> *Moving forward, our LPs will invest into The Sequoia Fund, an open-ended liquid portfolio made up of the public positions in a selection of our enduring companies. The Sequoia Fund will in turn allocate capital to a series of closed-end sub funds for venture investments at every stage from inception to IPO. Proceeds from these venture investments will flow back into The Sequoia Fund in a continuous feedback loop.*[10]

---

[10] https://medium.com/sequoia-capital/the-sequoia-fund-patient-capital-for-building-enduring-companies-9ed7bcd6c7da

---

Note   Government regulations can certainly have major impact
on investments. A case of this happened in the late 1970s. The
Department of Labor allowed for employee pension funds to not have
to abide by the "prudent man rule." The result was that they could
invest in riskier investments, such as venture capital funds.

VC firms are even looking at ways to expand into other parts of the
traditional financial services market. Again, Sequoia is a firm that has been
at the leading edge of this trend. With a large network of entrepreneurs and
employees that has become wealthy, the firm has set up its own wealth
management firm, called Heritage.

It has about $14 billion in assets under management and invests in
categories outside of venture investments.[11] The firm also manages money
for institutional investors.

Angel Investing

In 2010, Travis Kalanick raised $1.6 million for his startup, which was
called UberCab (the company would eventually be renamed Uber). At
the time, the focus was on providing an app for a ride-hailing service with
luxury black cars. The valuation of the startup was $5.4 million.[12]

Among the investors in the round was Alfred Lin. He was the chairman
and operating officer of Zappos, the online shoe e-tailer. He invested
$30,000. When he later joined Sequoia, he brought the deal to the partners.
But they passed on it. As for Lin's investment, it would be worth $149
million when Uber came public in 2019.

---

[11] www.ft.com/content/1024976f-5b97-4758-8322-3a37e644c33d

[12] www.wsj.com/articles/uber-jackpot-inside-one-of-the-greatest-
startup-investments-of-all-time-11557496421

Basically, Lin was an angel investor. That is, he was investing his own money in an early-stage startup. Such a person is an accredited investor. They may also be working full-time, such as a lawyer, doctor, real estate developer, corporate executive, founder, and so on.

And yes, the returns on angel investments can be huge. But there are considerable risks as well. The reality is that most angel investments wind up being losers. Moreover, when a deal does well, it will usually take years until you can monetize it – say five to ten years. This is why it is a good idea to invest in, say, 10 or more deals. This will help to reduce the risks of the portfolio. Keep in mind that angel investments follow the J-Curve.

Note   The potential for huge returns is certainly not the main benefit of angel investing. Note that it can be fun and exhilarating. You get to be a part of an exciting venture that may ultimately change the world. As an angel investor, you may even be a mentor to the founders.

An angel round usually comes after a friend-and-family funding and the amount ranges from $25,000 to $500,000. This is known as a seed or pre-seed round.

There are "super angels" – who are very wealthy individuals – who may write a check for the whole amount. But the usual case is for a group of angels to participate in a round and one or two of them will lead it.

There may be additional rounds so as to lessen the dilution. But it is more common for the next funding to be from venture capitalists. This would be a Series A round, which may be $5 million to $15 million or so.

Before making an investment, angels will usually have the entrepreneurs make a presentation. But evaluating the potential for the investment is far from easy. Because the startup is in the early phases, there will be minimal or no revenues. The company may actually be more of an idea or concept. Because of this, angels will look at the leadership skills, passion, and vision of the founders. It can really be a "gut decision."

Consider the story of Andy Bechtolsheim, who founded Sun Microsystems. In 1998, he met two students at Stanford – Sergey Brin and Larry Page. He saw the prototype of their search engine and invested $100,000 in Google. It was the company's first outside investment. According to Bechtolsheim: "So I really invested in the company to solve my own problem which was how to find information on the internet which in 1998 was actually a very difficult thing to do."[13]

When it comes to evaluating a startup investment, here are some factors to consider:

- TAM: While VCs look for $1+ billion opportunities, this may not be the case for an angel deal. If there are one or two rounds of angel financing and the startup winds up being sold within a few years, the returns can still be significant.

- Experience: It certainly helps if you have a background in what the startup does. This helps to better understand the opportunity. But you could provide more value-add in terms of advice as well as introductions to customers, partners, and employees.

- Skin-in-the-Game: It's encouraging that the founders have invested their own money in the startup. This is even if it is a small amount. The founders may not have much income or assets.

- Red Flags: Be wary when a founder makes claims that seem to be misguided or even wrong. Some of the typical ones are that the startup has no competition, or the projections are conservative.

---

[13] www.dw.com/en/von-bechtolsheim-i-invested-in-google-to-solve-my-own-problem/a-4557608

- Painkiller: A good analogy is the difference between vitamins and aspirin. While vitamins are helpful and can improve your health, they do not help with immediate pain. Of course, an aspirin does. In other words, you want a startup that is more like an aspirin, not a vitamin. This means that customers will be more willing to pay for the product or service.

- Due Diligence: This is the process of investigating the company. This is often done by using checklists. For example, you can look to see if there are well-written contracts, that the company owns its technologies, there are no lawsuits, the customer references are positive, and so on. Due diligence will also look at market factors, such as the size and competitive environment. Another good practice is to do an online background check on the founders. Do they have a criminal record?

Then what about the valuation of the startup? As we saw with VC deals, it can be a blend of art and science. But ultimately, it will come down to a negotiation between the parties.

There will be a pre-and-post money valuation. Let's take an example. Suppose you agree to invest in ABC Corp. at a valuation of $1 million. This is the pre-money valuation. For the investment, you write a check for $200,000. This puts the post-money valuation at $1.2 million, which is the $1 million pre-money valuation plus the $200,000 investment.

Note   There are various online calculators to estimate the valuation of startups. An example is canyon.com/valuation.php.

When an investor wants to make an investment, they will put together a term sheet and provide it to the startup. The document is not long, say under ten pages. But it sets forth the key terms of the deal like the valuation, the amount of the capital, the type of equity or debt involved, and the conditions. For example, it is common that the term sheet is valid so long as there are no material problems found in the due diligence process.

Founders like to use term sheets to shop their deal. They will show them to other investors to gin up more interest – driving up the valuation. As a result, an investor will put a time limit on the term sheet. This can be a few days.

After the signing of the term sheet, there will be the due diligence process and negotiation of the deal documents. A big part of this will be the drafting of the representations and warranties. These essentially mean that the parties stand by their claims.

In this process, if there are problems that emerge, this may not mean the deal is nixed. Rather, it is more common for the parties to renegotiate the terms. This could mean reducing the valuation.

In terms of the security that the investor gets, this can vary. It may be common stock or preferred stock. Although, the typical security is a convertible note. This is an IOU, which converts into the company's equity.

Why do this? The main reason is that it is much simpler, such as in terms of the legal documents and regulatory issues. In fact, incubators like YCominator have open sourced their own documents for convertible debt (`www.ycombinator.com/documents/`).

The holder of a convertible note will get a discount that can range from 10% to 30% or so. This means that – when there is another round of funding or an acquisition—the investor will convert the shares at a lower price.

But there is a flaw with this. For example, suppose you invest $50,000 in ABC Corp. when the valuation is at $1 million, and you get a convertible note with a 30% discount. Then a year later, the company gets a Series A round for $30 million at a $100 million valuation. In this case, you will convert your note at a high valuation of $70 million.

To avoid this, you can negotiate for a cap on the convertible note. This is where there will be a maximum valuation. In our example, this could be something like $1 million.

Deal Flow

Super angels like Ron Conway, Peter Theil, and Reid Hoffman have extensive networks. This means that they see many top-notch deals. In a sense, they are gatekeepers.

But you do not have to be a super angel to get deal flow. Here are some suggestions:

- LinkedIn: This can be a great way to find potential deals.

- Social Media: Being active on Twitter and Facebook can give you more visibility within the startup world. Another good idea is to set up your own blog.

- Events: There are a myriad of startup conferences and business plan contests. They can be a great way to find deals and build your network.

As you engage in various angel deals, you will start to build a reputation. Other entrepreneurs will talk to their friends and refer you. What's more, the investors you work with as well as advisors, like lawyers and CPAs, will be a source of deal flow.

Although, one of the best ways to expand your opportunities is to join an angel network. This is an organization that will host presentations from startup founders. For those deals that look interesting, some of the angels will take the lead and bring other investors on board.

Table 5-1 shows some of the top angel networks.

Table 5-1. *Angel Networks*

Firms
Tech Coast Angels (https://www.techcoastangels.com/)
New York Angels (https://www.newyorkangels.com/)
Band of Angels (https://www.bandangels.com/)
Pasadena Angels (https://www.pasadenaangels.com/)
Golden Seeds (https://goldenseeds.com/)
Sand Hill Angels (https://www.sandhillangels.com/)
Boston Harbor Angels (https://www.bostonharborangels.com/)

Another option is to join an incubator or accelerator. These organizations usually focus on startups at a very early stage. The incubator and accelerator will provide mentoring to improve on the business. Then there will be a Demo Day, which investors will attend. At this stage, the investment levels are usually small – say $25,000 to $100,000.

Note   The origin of "angel" as an investor actually came in the early 1900s. This described a person who provided financing for plays.

Equity Crowdfunding

When a company wants to issue equity, the process can be time-consuming and expensive. This is especially the case for an IPO. A company needs to register its securities with the Securities and Exchange Commission.

Consider that private companies can avoid this. How so? Basically, it involves mostly issuing the securities to accredited investors.

However, this may not be a good solution for early-stage startups. The founders may not have access to a network of accredited investors. Or, if they do, it can be tough to convince them to invest in the venture.

This is why Congress passed the Jumpstart Our Business Startups (JOBS) Act in 2012. The legislation greatly reduced the requirements for raising equity capital. It also allowed for a company to use an online portal to sell shares.

Here are some of the rules:

- A company can raise up to $5 million during a 12-month period.

- A company must provide complete and accurate disclosures to investors to make informed decisions. While the laws are less stringent, the companies still must abide by the anti-fraud statutes.

- A company must be based in the United States.

- The minimum investments can be low, say $50 per deal.

- If you're a non-accredited investor, there are restrictions on how much you can invest. This is the greater of $2,200 or 5% of the greater of your annual income or net worth (if either is less than $107,000), or 10% of the greater of your annual income or net worth.

The total cannot exceed $107,000. You must disclose this information on all crowdfunding portals you sign up for.

- An investor must be at least 18 years old.

There are many online crowdfunding platforms. But it's best to use those that have the following characteristics:

- Strong backing: This would be investment from venture capitalists or private equity firms. Or the crowdfunding platform could be owned by a larger company. This should allow for more resources and stronger safeguards for investors.

- Deal Flow: Look for those that have a lot of deals on the site, say over 50.

- Compliance: A crowdfunding portal must be registered with the SEC and a member of FINRA (Financial Industry Regulatory Authority).

A crowdfunding site will have listings of various deals.

You then click on a deal and will get a detailed profile. Some of the materials include the investor presentation, terms of the transaction, investor documents, online forums, updates, and so on.

Even though some crowdfunding platforms will provide due diligence to screen deals, you should still do your own research. You can do Google searchers on the team, analyze the competition, and identify the potential risks.

A crowdfunding deal may have different types of equity, whether common stock, preferred stock, or convertible notes. Although, the most common is convertible notes.

Note   Some of the top equity crowdfunding platforms include SeedInvest, Republic, WeFunder, NetCapital, MicroVentures, and StartEngine.

There are different fee arrangements. They range from processing and payments fees to getting a percentage of the amount raised.

After you make an investment, you can track them via a dashboard. You should also get access to annual or quarterly reports.

Publicly Traded Private Equity Firms

A way to get exposure to private equity is to invest in the firms that manage funds. During the past decade, some of the world's largest have come public. Table 5-2 shows a list.

Table 5-2. *Top publicly traded private equity firms*

Firms	Assets
Blackstone	$731 billion
KKR	$460 billion
Apollo Global management	$481 billion
Carlyle Group	$290 billion
TPG	$109 billion

The top firms started with buyouts. But over the years, they have branched out into other categories like real estate, credit, and growth equity. In other words, these firms have diversified revenue bases.

However, the performance can be volatile. Part of this is due to the swings in the markets. Next, the valuations of portfolio companies can be unpredictable since they rely on the timing of IPOs and acquisitions. Finally, another key factor is the growth in assets under management. This provides higher management fees as well as the potential for more revenues from the carried interest.

In fact, to boost assets under management, some private equity firms have been acquiring insurance companies. During the past couple years, Apollo Global Management acquired Athene Holding for $11 billion,[14] and KKR purchased Global Atlantic Financial Group for $4.4 billion.[15]

Conclusion

Private equity is a big category, and it is becoming more important for finding ways to get higher returns. A key part of this is the active involvement of the portfolio managers. With buyout funds, they own the business and try to find ways to boost value. As for venture capital funds, the partners will help with the business model, getting customers, and recruiting.

Angel investing is another way to participate in private equity. But this is mostly for early-stage deals. While they can be risky, the returns can be significant.

Then there is equity crowdfunding. This is a much easier way to participate in early-stage companies. But again, it's important to do your own research.

As for the next chapter, we'll take a look at crypto.

---

[14] www.apollo.com/media/press-releases/2021/03-08-2021-120032339
[15] www.willkie.com/news/2020/07/kkr-acquires-global-atlantic-financial-group

CHAPTER 6

Crypto

Digital Currencies, NFTs, and DeFi

> *Bitcoin's structure is very ingenious. The paper money disappears, and cryptocurrencies are a much better way to transfer values than a piece of paper, that's for sure.*

—Elon Musk

In May 2021, tech entrepreneur Elon Musk hosted *Saturday Night Live*. In his monologue, he said: "To anyone I've offended I just want to say: I reinvented electric cars and I'm sending people to Mars in a rocket ship ... did you also think I was going to be a chill, normal dude?"[1]

He then did a variety of sketches, such as about a Gen Z hospital, a western and a parody of the movie, *The Martian*. He also riffed about cryptocurrencies, such as dogecoin. He actually said it was a "hustle" and the value of it would go on to plunge.

---

[1] www.theguardian.com/tv-and-radio/2021/may/09/saturday-night-live-elon-musk

© Tom Taulli 2022
T. Taulli, *The Personal Finance Guide for Tech Professionals*,
https://doi.org/10.1007/978-1-4842-8242-7_6

115

Musk's appearance was another indication that cryptocurrencies were becoming mainstream. In other words, they are something investors should know about.

This is what we'll cover in this chapter. We'll look at how cryptocurrencies work, the ways to invest in them, and how to evaluate the risks.

What Is Crypto?

Crypto is short for cryptocurrency. This is a digital currency that is decentralized. There is no central authority – like a government entity – that controls it. It is instead controlled by a network of computers, which are called nodes.

You can use cryptocurrency to make a purchase and sell an item. However, there are still many merchants that do not accept this form of payment. So instead, cryptocurrency is often a form of investment. Investors will essentially buy it like a stock or a bond.

The most common cryptocurrency is Bitcoin, which was launched in January 2009. But since then, there have emerged thousands more that have hit the markets. The total value is over $3 trillion.

Why the popularity of crypto? Here are some reasons:

- Distrust in institutions: It should be no surprise that Bitcoin was developed during the financial crisis. This was a period when millions of people lost faith in their banks. There was also distrust of government institutions. With crypto, the belief was that there would be more protection against manipulation, such as with inflation. After all, governments have the power to print money. But many cryptocurrencies have coded limits on the number of digital coins.

- Digital Future: It's clear that the megatrend is toward digital assets and payments as most people have smartphones to make transactions. It is also much more convenient to use them for financial activities.

- Speculation: Crypto has become a way to generate substantial wealth – at least for some people.

- Intermediaries: There are none for crypto. You do not need a financial institution to process a transaction. It is all handled with the decentralized computer network – on a 24/7 basis. The decentralization also means your cryptocurrency is portable. You can keep it wherever you want.

- Privacy: When you make a payment with a cryptocurrency, you do not have to provide your personal information to a merchant.

- Access: Billions of people lack access to basic financial services. But crypto has democratized things.

- Cross-Border Transactions: Using traditional systems, these payments can take days and have high fees. But crypto is transformative. A transaction can take minutes and be at a fraction of the cost.

Blockchain is another critical reason for the popularity of crypto. This technology allows for decentralized management of transactions, which are transparent and virtually impossible to manipulate. Think of it as a digital ledger. For each transaction, there is an individual block that contains information, and the nodes in the network will verify it. Since each node has a copy of the blockchain, there is no problem if one of the nodes break down. This is why it would be extremely difficult for a government to shut it down.

Then how does the validation work? It involves solving complicated math problems. These include different approaches like Proof-of-work (PoW) – which is used by Bitcoin, Dogecoin, Litecoin, and so on – or Proof-of-stake (PoS), which tends to be less energy intensive with computer resources. Cryptocurrencies that use this are Cardano, Ethereum 2.0, and Polkadot. For the node that gets the correct answer, it will receive an incentive like extra cryptocurrency. Such a node is called a miner.

Transferring cryptocurrency involves a process referred to as cryptography (this is where the word "crypto" comes from). It is where information is encrypted and decrypted to provide for high levels of security. To do this, there are public and private keys, which use long strings of characters. The public key is visible to everybody and provides a location for the cryptocurrency. As for the private key, this is essentially a password that allows access to the blockchain. This provides you with ownership of the asset.

This presents a problem, though. If you lose the private key, you will likely be unable to do anything with your cryptocurrency. A tragic case of this was Gerald Cotton, who was the owner of Canada's largest cryptocurrency exchange. In 2018, he died but had not provided anyone with his private key. It meant that £145 million of cryptocurrency was inaccessible and roughly £41m belonged to customers.[2]

---

[2] www.independent.co.uk/life-style/gadgets-and-tech/news/bitcoin-exchange-quadrigacx-password-cryptocurrency-scam-a8763676.html

---

Note   On May 22, 2010, Laszlo Hanyecz made the first official
Bitcoin transaction. He used 10,000 coins to purchase two pizzas
from Papa John's. If he had not done this and kept the Bitcoin, they
would be worth over $300 million.[3]

The Market Size

Because of the volatility in the crypto market, the overall size can change
drastically. In 2021, the total valuation hit nearly $3 trillion, up from under
$1 trillion.[4] But then there was a sell-off, which took the market down to
$2.2 trillion.

According to a Pew Research study, about 16% of Americans have
invested in cryptocurrency.[5] The survey showed that the results skewed
toward males between the ages of 18 to 29.

The topic of crypto is mostly universal as well. The Pew study shows
that 86% of Americans have heard of it. This compares to 48% in 2015.
At the time, only 1% had invested in crypto.

Given the popularity and demand for the cryptocurrencies, venture
capital firms have been ramping up their investments in the space.

---

[3] www.yahoo.com/now/bitcoin-pizza-day-sees-first-112000121.
html#:~:text=2010%2C%20Florida%20Man%20Laszlo%20Hanyecz,transaction%20
with%20an%20actual%20company.

[4] www.wsj.com/articles/nfts-and-snl-crypto-keeps-burrowing-into-the-
mainstream-11640567423

[5] www.pewresearch.org/fact-tank/2021/11/11/16-of-americans-say-they-
have-ever-invested-in-traded-or-used-cryptocurrency/

In 2021, they poured over $27 billion in funding across the globe.[6] This was more than all the investments for the prior decade. Much of the funding has been focused on building the core infrastructure of crypto. Some crypto exchanges, like Crypto.com and Coinbase, have formed their own venture funds so as to help bolster the ecosystem.

Interestingly, there is still much concentration of the wealth in the crypto market. Analysis from the National Bureau of Economic Research shows that 0.01% of the Bitcoin owners – out of about 114 million – control roughly 27% of the 19 million coins in circulation.[7]

Volatility

If there is one common feature of cryptocurrency, it is volatility. It can be extreme at times, even for the top coins like Bitcoin. Thus, before investing in cryptocurrency, it's important to understand the risks. You could quickly lose money!

Take a look at Bitcoin in 2021. It got off to a strong start. One of the catalysts was Elon Musk, who added #bitcoin to his Twitter bio. He has over 70 million followers.

Then on a Sunday, Bitcoin plunged 20%. Yet by the end of the first quarter, it had more than doubled. But then Bitcoin would go into reverse and lose half its value during the next few months.

Then what came after this? Well, it pulled off another double. But by the end of the year, there was a sell-off – and this continued into 2022.

---

[6] www.nytimes.com/2021/12/01/business/dealbook/crypto-venture-capital.html

[7] www.wsj.com/articles/bitcoins-one-percent-controls-lions-share-of-the-cryptocurrencys-wealth-11639996204?mod=lead_feature_below_a_pos1

There were also times when the exchanges went haywire. For example, at one point, CoinMarketCap quoted a price of Bitcoin at $850 billion.[8] Of course, it was a glitch in the software and was fixed quickly.

Yes, 2021 was stomach churning and the crypto market remains the Wild Wild West. But interestingly enough, the year was milder than prior ones.

Note   Various crypto companies have been investing aggressively to make their brands mainstream. Look at Crypto.com. In 2021, the company agreed to a $700 million deal – for a 20-year term – for the naming rights to the Staples Center. This is where the Lakers and Clippers NBA teams play.[9]

How to Buy Crypto?

Buying and selling cryptocurrency is fairly easy. It's similar to an online brokerage account.

First of all, you will need to choose a platform. This can either be a cryptocurrency exchange, traditional brokerage, or a payments system like PayPal or Square. Some of the top exchanges include Coinbase, Gemini, Crypto.com, FTX, and Binance.

---

[8] www.barrons.com/articles/bitcoin-ether-prices-coinbase-coinmarketcap-51639789065?mod=hp_DAY_3

[9] www.wsj.com/articles/staples-center-in-l-a-to-be-renamed-crypto-com-arena-11637145428

It's a good idea to research different options. After all, some will have a limited number of cryptocurrencies to trade. The fees can also vary widely. They can be levied on the deposits and withdrawals as well as the trading. There are also fees for borrowing against your account.

In the United States, many of the top cryptocurrency exchanges are not decentralized. This means you must provide your identification information when you sign up for an account. For example, with Coinbase, you need to enter the following:

- Proof you are at least 18 years old

- A government-issued photo ID

- A phone number connected to your smartphone

You want to make sure your account is as secure as possible. To this end, you should have a strong password – with a mix of lowercase and uppercase letters, numbers, and special characters – and use two-factor authentication.

Next, you will need to use a payment option to fund your account. Many exchanges accept bank accounts, debit cards, and credit cards. Although, you should first check with your financial services company. Some will have restrictions or limits when making transfers for cryptocurrency.

Once your account is set up, you can then make transactions. It's a matter of a few clicks to buy and sell cryptocurrencies. Many exchanges also allow for different types of orders, such as limits and stop losses. There may also be ways to set up recurring purchase programs. This can be a good way to build a position in a cryptocurrency.

Note   Some cryptocurrencies like Bitcoin sell for thousands of dollars. But if this is too much for you, you can still buy fractional amounts, say at $25.

There is no limit to how much cryptocurrency you can sell. However, if you transfer the money to your bank account, there may be daily or monthly withdrawal limits.

Note that cryptocurrency investments do not have the protection of the Securities Investor Protection Corporation (SIPC), which is for brokerage accounts of up to $500,000 and cash of $250,000. This program allows for the backing of your account if there is the liquidation of the firm. But depending on the cryptocurrency exchange, the cash balances may be protected by FDIC insurance (up to $250,000 per account).

Yet a cryptocurrency exchange may have insurance for hacking. But this does not include the theft of passwords.

When you own cryptocurrency, you will store it in a digital wallet (this essentially holds the private keys). This can be part of an exchange. But if you want more control and perhaps more safety, you may instead want to use a third-party wallet. Here are the two main options:

- Hot Wallets: These are on the cloud. True, this is convenient, allowing you access from your computer, phone, or tablet. But there is still the potential for a hack. Again, this is why it is a good idea to have a strong password and two-factor authentication.

- Cold Wallets: These are wallets that are disconnected from the Internet. The simplest cold wallet is actually using paper! Some people may even laminate this and keep it in a safety deposit box. Another type of cold wallet is a hardware device like a USB drive. This means there is minimal connection to the Internet. Some of the top providers of cold wallets are Ledger and Trezor.

Note   A Bitcoin ATM is like a regular ATM. You can make in-person transactions with cryptocurrencies.[10] Even Walmart is doing this with its Coinstar kiosks.[11]

Types of Crypto

The crypto world can move quickly. There are also new coins created frequently.

But what are some of the main cryptocurrencies? Let's take a look:

- Bitcoin: This is the largest on the global market. It has the advantage of a long track record and brand recognition. If anything, the word Bitcoin is often synonymous with cryptocurrency. In 2021, Tesla acquired $1.5 billion in Bitcoin in order to accept it for the payment for its cars.[12]

- Ether: This is the No. 2 cryptocurrency. The foundation of ether is Ethereum, which is the most used blockchain, which allows for smart contracts and NFTs. Another benefit is that it is more energy efficient and quicker.

---

[10] www.yahoo.com/now/bitcoin-pizza-day-sees-first-112000121. html#:~:text=2010%2C%20Florida%20Man%20Laszlo%20Hanyecz,transaction%20 with%20an%20actual%20company.

[11] www.coindesk.com/business/2021/10/21/walmart-has-quietly-begun-hosting-bitcoin-atms/

[12] www.cnbc.com/2021/04/28/tesla-is-now-sitting-on-2point5-billion-of-bitcoin.html

- Cardano: The cofounder of Ethereum, Charles Hoskinson, launched this in 2017. A major advantage to Cardano is speed – at one million transactions per second – which is better than Ethereum. It also allows for the building of decentralized applications (dApps). This allows for creating systems for lending, depositing, and transfers.

- Solana: This cryptocurrency is quick but also has a low fee structure. This is especially the case when compared to Ethereum. This has helped Solona get to wide adoption. Note that the transaction fees can be at a fraction of a penny.

- Litecoin: This is one of the older cryptocurrencies, which was founded in 2011. The inventor of this coin – Google engineer Charlie Lee – wanted to improve upon some of the weaknesses of Bitcoin, such as the lengthiness of the verification process. It's essentially a "lite" version of Bitcoin.

- Polkadot: One of the drawbacks of cryptocurrencies is that they often do not operate on different blockchains. So the purpose of Polkadot is to solve this problem. As a validation of this cryptocurrency, Deutsche Telekom bought a "significant" amount of Polkadot tokens in 2021.[13]

---

[13] www.coindesk.com/business/2021/12/21/polkadot-is-deutsche-telekoms-latest-crypto-experiment/

- Tether: This is popular stablecoin. This means that the cryptocurrency is pegged to the value of the US dollar. This is to reduce volatility so as to make it easier for people to make real-world transactions.

Valuing Crypto

The valuation of crypto is far from easy. It's just really a bunch of code.

Yet there are some factors to consider. First of all, the value of crypto is helped by factors like speed and low costs. This helps with the spread of the coin. Another key is the limit on how much of the cryptocurrency can be mined. This creates scarcity. In the case of Bitcoin, a maximum of 21 million can be created.

Next, influencers can have a major impact on the value of cryptocurrency. A prime example is Musk. One tweet from him can drive the value of a cryptocurrency.

However, there are long-term considerations. This is the case if there is adoption and investment from major companies. For example, the upgrades of the traditional credit card networks – from Visa and MasterCard – for cryptocurrencies is critical.

Something else to note is the overall usefulness of the cryptocurrency. Can the underlying technology be used for applications other than finance? If so, this should make the cryptocurrency more valuable.

Then there are macroeconomic factors. As noted earlier, cryptocurrencies have been deemed to be hedges against inflation.

Although, since these digital assets are still new, it is not clear how durable these relationships are. When inflation spiked in 2021, many cryptocurrencies actually fell! Then again, this may have been due to the Federal Reserve's tighter monetary policy, which reduced liquidity in the system. Bottom line: macroeconomic impacts are extremely complicated.

But ultimately, when it comes to the value of a cryptocurrency, it's about what someone else is willing to buy or sell it at. Yes, it comes down to the proverbial "supply and demand" – and this can be quite volatile with emerging digital assets.

There are definitely crypto skeptics, such as Citadel's Ken Griffin. In an interview with the New York Times, he discussed the difficulties with valuing cryptocurrencies.[14] He noted there are no tried-and-true metrics that exist with other asset classes like common stocks and bonds. For example, the valuations are based on models that evaluate cash flows.

He also believes that cryptocurrencies lack good fraud protection, which could limit their uses as a medium of exchange. He used the analogy of the traditional credit card. If someone steals and uses it to make purchases, you will likely be made whole. But what if this happens with your cryptocurrencies? Well, you will likely be out of luck.

Note   In 2021, hedge fund investor Ken Griffin paid $43.2 million for a first-edition copy of the US Constitution.[15] He made the bid at a Sotheby's auction, which lasted eight minutes. He beat out a group of 17,000 crypto investors who crowdfunded $40 million.

---

[14] www.youtube.com/watch?v=yF-WTRoSPhg

[15] www.cnbc.com/2021/11/19/citadel-ceo-ken-griffin-pays-43point2-million-for-constitution-copy-outbidding-crypto-group.html

DeFi

DeFi is short for decentralized finance. This is an emerging group of technologies and systems that leverage blockchain technologies for peer-to-peer financial services. These include payments, lending, insurance, cross-border transactions, and so on. Think of DeFi as the crypto versions of traditional financial services, such as a bank or brokerage.

For now, the main public blockchain for this is Ethereum. This allows for the creation of sophisticated dApps. But there are other contending platforms.

A benefit of DeFi is the automation. There is no need to have offices, trading floors, or bank branches. The transactions are processed across the peer-to-peer network, which should greatly lower the costs and allow for higher speeds.

To become a member of a DeFi network, you need to have a digital wallet (it connects to a dApp). This will provide you with instantaneous access to the services. You do not even have to provide your email, name, or other personal information. Any asset you deposit with a dApp is called your total value locked.

Here are some other benefits of DeFi:

- Interest is earned every minute, not on a monthly basis.

- You can get a loan without filling out huge amounts of paperwork. These are called "flash loans."

- The interest rates are usually higher than for traditional bank accounts and money market funds.

- You can use derivatives like stock options and futures with DeFi.

The growth of DeFi has been staggering. In 2021, the spending went from $19 billion to $243 billion, according to DeFi Llama.[16] A big part of this was for users that borrowed against their crypto holdings.

But there are considerable risks. Some DeFi platforms make it possible to borrow huge amounts, which can be 100 times your collateral. This can amplify your returns. But if your trades go against you, it does not take much to lose substantial amounts. You may ultimately lose everything. In fact, this heavy leverage is one of the reasons for the volatility for cryptocurrencies.

The DeFi platforms are mostly unregulated and there is no insurance for fraud or bankrupt firms. Some of the companies are even anonymous, making it nearly impossible to do research on them.

In 2021, Chainalysis reported there was $14 billion in cryptocurrency fraud – up 79% on a year-over-year basis – and much of it was due to DeFi platforms.[17] Note that the code base for dApps has vulnerabilities to hacking. According to the Chainalysis report: "But DeFi is unlikely to realize its full potential if the same decentralization that makes it so dynamic also allows for widespread scamming and theft."

Note   In a New York Times interview, Apple CEO Tim Cook said he owns cryptocurrency. He noted: "I think it's reasonable to own it as part of a diversified portfolio. I'm not giving anyone investment advice by the way." He also said he has been interested in cryptocurrency "for a while."[18]

---

[16] https://defillama.com/

[17] www.cnbc.com/2022/01/06/crypto-scammers-took-a-record-14-billion-in-2021-chainalysis.html

[18] www.cnbc.com/2021/11/09/apple-ceo-tim-cook-says-he-owns-cryptocurrency.html

NFTs

An NFT is short for a non-fungible token. Sounds kind of weird. This is true. But the "non-fungible" part means that an NFT is unique and cannot be replaced by something else. Think of it as an original painting from Picasso – but it is in digital form.

By comparison, a cryptocurrency is fungible. For example, a Bitcoin is no different from another one. Or a traditional dollar bill is fungible. You can use any one to make a transaction.

The core technology behind NFTs is the Ethereum blockchain. It has a system that is special to create unique tokens.

Some examples of NFTs are visuals of artworks, trading cards, video skins in games, tweets, and even fractional ownership of real estate. In the future, this technology could be used for applications, for say, identification for a driver's license or passport.

There are many marketplaces where you can purchase NFTs like OpenSea, Nifty Gateway, and Mintable. Like a crypto exchange, they will charge a fee, which could be a percentage of the value of the NFT.

You definitely need to do your own research. It's a good idea to use those marketplaces that have strong backing from reputable sources, such as venture capitalists. You will also need a digital wallet to make the purchase.

You can make your own NFTs and sell them. The process is actually easy. A marketplace will have a place to upload your own material and there will then be some steps for the NFT conversion.

The NFT market certainly hit an inflection point in 2021. The volume of activity hit $44.2 billion, according to Chainalysis.[19] Note that a large amount of the transactions were for under $10,000 on cryptocurrency.

---

[19] https://blog.chainalysis.com/reports/nft-market-report-preview-2021/

It's not uncommon for certain collections of NFTs to quickly get hot and then cold. The market is still very much in the experimental stage and involves many retail investors. Data from the OpenSea marketplace shows that under 30% of minted NFT transactions are profitable.[20]

Yet some of the transactions can be quite large. Consider the example of Mike Winkelmann, who is a digital artist called Beeple. One of his JPG NFTs – which was a collage of digital images – sold for $69.3 million at a Christie's online auction in March 2021.[21]

A strategy to boost the value of an NFT is whitelisting. This involves aggressive promotion on social platforms like Discord and Twitter. To create the buzz, the NFT creator will reward users with the opportunity to buy new NFTs at discounted prices.

Given the importance of building audiences, celebrities and athletes have become early adopters of NFTs. Consider famed quarterback Tom Brady. He co-founded Autograph, which is an NFT agency. The firm helps top athletes better manage their NFT efforts. It uses the Polygon blockchain, which is based on the Ethereum infrastructure. But it relies on much less energy. In 2021, Autograph announced a $170 million Series A round led by Andreessen Horowitz and Kleiner Perkins.[22]

---

[20] https://cryptonews.com/news/only-1-in-4-nfts-bought-during-minting-result-in-profit-chainalysis.htm

[21] www.nytimes.com/2021/03/11/arts/design/nft-auction-christies-beeple.html

[22] https://techcrunch.com/2022/01/19/tom-bradys-buzzy-celebrity-nft-startup-autograph-banks-170m-from-silicon-valleys-top-crypto-investors/

Sports leagues are even making a play for the market. The NBA teamed up with Dapper Labs to launch Top Shot. It's a platform to buy NFTs from professional basketball players.[23]

Note   In March 2021, Kings of Lean was the first band to release an album as an NFT.[24] It was called *When You See Yourself*. The band included a series of NFTs, which came with perks like front-row seats for life.

When you purchase an NFT, you have two ways to prove your ownership. There is the private key and the image that is uploaded to the public digital ledger of the blockchain.

Now just because you own the NFT does not mean you are the owner of the underlying object. This is a matter of copyright law. For example, if I turned my book into an NFT and you purchased it, you would own the unique digital item. But I would still own the copyright to the material in the book.

Regulations

Whenever there is a new technology that emerges, the legal system will be slow to regulate it. This is certainly the case with crypto. It is still relatively new and changing rapidly.

---

[23] www.wsj.com/articles/ethereum-is-booming-in-the-nft-frenzyso-is-network-congestion-11620050853

[24] www.rollingstone.com/pro/news/kings-of-leon-when-you-see-yourself-album-nft-crypto-1135192/

But in the coming years, there will be more regulations, laws, and restrictions on the market. On the one hand, this will increase costs and prevent certain types of activities. Although, there will be benefits. The legal requirements will provide more safety – and also encourage larger organizations to participate.

But regulating crypto is far from easy. Unlike traditional financial services, the industry does not have intermediaries. So it is not clear who should be responsible.

Yet there are still players in the crypto ecosystem that have qualities of an intermediary. An example is the maintainers. They are coders who can make changes when there are bugs in the software.

Even if there are clear regulations, the enforcement will be challenging. The blockchains are complex and global. It can be easy for someone to, instead, make transactions in other countries that have looser regulations.

Now one place to start with regulations is to focus on the crypto exchanges. These handle large amounts of the transactions and also work with many users. Regulations can be helpful in providing standards, protections for assets, and more transparency.

Another issue is which US regulatory authorities would have jurisdiction. The fact is that there is a myriad of state and federal agencies – and they often have overlapping powers. For example, the banking industry is under the regulations of the Federal Reserve, the Office of the Comptroller of the Currency, and state authorities.

Also, with crypto, it is important to determine what type of asset it is. Is it like a currency, derivative, or a security like a common stock? If it is a security, then the Securities and Exchange Commission (SEC) would likely have the power. Or, if it is really a derivative, then the Commodity Futures Trading Commission would be the better option.

Ultimately, there will probably need to be a legislation from Congress. It may even involve the creation of a new agency that would be better equipped to deal with crypto.

But interestingly enough, such moves may not happen until there is a major implosion, such as a crash in the markets. For example, this was the catalyst for the wide-scale legislation for federal securities regulations during the 1930s.

Despite all the uncertainty, US regulatory agencies have been taking actions against various crypto organizations and investors. The SEC did this with lawsuits against companies that engaged in initial coin offerings. The agency believed that these were the issuance of unregistered securities and, as a result, violated the federal laws.

The US Department of Treasury is also getting more aggressive in regulating the crypto market. The agency has made a proposal to apply the so-called "travel rule." This means there will need to be disclosures of transactions in excess of $3,000.

A key motivation for governments to impose regulations is to protect their own powers. If there is widespread use of cryptocurrencies, then central banks like the Federal Reserve would have less impact in their policies. This is perhaps a reason China has banned transactions and mining of cryptocurrencies.

Taxes

The tax treatment of crypto is a specialized and complex area. A big part of this is due to the uncertainty of regulations.

As a result, it's a good idea to get the help of a tax professional. But there are still some concepts you need to understand as well as some steps to take.

First of all, you need to be diligent with your recordkeeping. This can be tough if you have different wallets, though. But one idea is to create a spreadsheet that lists the transactions and provides the profits and losses on the trades (your tax professional may already have one). Keep in mind that this is what you will need to fill out your 1040 tax return.

The IRS considers cryptocurrencies to be property not a currency. This means that you may be taxed for short- and long-term capital gains. You can also deduct losses. However, if you use crypto to buy a car, you may actually have to pay a tax on this transaction!

An NFT, though, may have different tax treatment. It appears that the IRS may consider this to be a collectible – like a piece of art, baseball card, or an antique – and this means that the top federal tax rate would be 31.8%.[25] By comparison, a gain on a cryptocurrency would be 23.8%.

For the 2021 Infrastructure legislation, Congress instituted some new tax regulations for cryptocurrencies and NFTs. There is a requirement that brokers list transactions on a 1099 form. However, this regulation will not come into effect until January 2024.[26]

Currently, the "wash rule" does not apply to cryptocurrency transactions. The wash rule means you cannot deduct this loss unless you buy back the security or something similar to it after 30 days.

But Congress has been looking at imposing the wash rule on the crypto market. It was actually a part of President Biden's Build Back Better legislation.

OK then, can you buy cryptocurrency in a retirement account and get the deduction? It's not clear cut. But there are various firms – like ForUsAll, BitcoinIRA, and Kingdom Trust – that provide crypto as an investment option for 401(k)s and IRAs.[27]

---

[25] www.cnbc.com/2022/01/11/make-a-killing-on-nfts-and-crypto-the-irs-may-tax-them-differently.html

[26] www.cnbc.com/2021/12/28/how-to-prepare-for-2022-tax-season-and-potential-crypto-regulation.html

[27] www.wsj.com/articles/saving-for-retirement-now-you-can-bet-on-bitcoin-11624613435

Note   A 1040 tax return asks the question: "At any time during [the year], did you receive, sell, exchange, or otherwise dispose of any financial interest in any virtual currency?" If you did so but answer No then you could be in trouble if the IRS audits your return. You may be subject to back taxes, interest, and penalties.

Crypto ETFs

In the United States, you cannot buy an ETF that directly owns cryptocurrencies. The SEC has been resistant to approve funds in this category because of the potential risks.

However, there are a variety of ETFs that trade futures contracts on cryptocurrencies. These are instruments similar to options that have high levels of leverage and trade on the CME (Chicago Mercantile Exchange). In other words, they can be even more volatile than owning cryptocurrencies.

Yet the ETFs try to reduce this by purchasing futures contracts with short maturities. This is the case with the ProShares Bitcoin Strategy ETF (BITO) or the VanEck Bitcoin Strategy ETF (XBTF).

Yet these ETFs have high fees, such as expense ratios of close to 1%. There are also the costs a fund will incur for having to frequently replace futures contracts.

To avoid some of the problems, there are crypto funds that are structured as closed-end funds. A leader in the category is Grayscale Bitcoin Trust, which tracks the value of Bitcoin according to the CoinDesk Bitcoin Price Index. But it usually trades at a discount to its NAV. This means that the value of the shares will not track the cryptocurrency in lock step. The expense ratio is also fairly high, at 2%.

Another option is to buy an ETF that invests in stocks that have exposure to cryptocurrency and blockchain. This means investing in companies like crypto miners, exchanges, or tech firms.

A notable ETF in the space is Amplify Transformational Data Sharing ETF (BLOK). It is actively managed and owns miners like Marathon Digital and exchanges, such as Coinbase (as of the first quarter of 2022). But it also has investments in other ETFs.

Note   In the summer of 2021, El Salvador became the first country to make Bitcoin legal tender for transactions. But the US dollar remains the primary currency.

Conclusion

In a relatively short period of time, crypto has become an important part of the investment world. It is no longer a niche. Some of the world's top financial firms are investing in this market as well as some of the wealthiest individuals.

But crypto is likely to remain volatile. There are also not many safeguards. Thus, the risks are high. So before you invest in crypto, you need to do your own homework.

The regulatory framework remains in flux. And there could easily be more restrictions in the coming years. But this should ultimately be a positive. It will allow for a more normal marketplace.

Then there is the emergence of DeFi, which offers a next-generation approach to financial services. NFTs are also interesting, providing investors with a way to buy unique digital items.

As for the next chapter, we'll take a look at hard assets.

CHAPTER 7

Hard Assets

Real Estate, Commodities, and Art

Buy land, they aren't making it anymore.

—Mark Twain[1]

Hard assets are tangible and include real estate, commodities, artwork, collectibles, and so on. This is the oldest asset class.

Investing in hard assets has traditionally been for those who are wealthy. Such investments may require large investment amounts and ongoing maintenance.

But with the emergence of online platforms and ETFs, it is much easier to participate in hard assets nowadays. This type of investment also has many advantages.

In this chapter, we'll take a closer look at hard assets and how they can improve your returns.

---

[1] www.jbeardcompany.com/buy-land-arent-making-anymore-mark-twain/

© Tom Taulli 2022
T. Taulli, *The Personal Finance Guide for Tech Professionals*,
https://doi.org/10.1007/978-1-4842-8242-7_7

Why Invest in Hard Assets?

The future growth opportunities for hard assets look promising. Keep in mind that there are a variety of megatrends that should increase demand. Let's take a look:

- Global Growth: The world's population continues to grow at a rapid pace. In 1950, there were about 2.6 billion people. Since then, it has reached about 7.9 billion. The United Nations forecasts that the global population will hit 9.7 billion by 2050 and 11 billion by 2100.[2] Some of the drivers for the growth include higher fertility rates, better healthcare, and increased urbanization. Going forward, more than half of the population growth will be in Africa. In light of all this, there will be substantial increases in demand for land – whether for homes, offices, manufacturing, or agriculture – as well as commodities and energy. Population growth is perhaps the most important factor for hard assets.

- Institutional Interest: Hedge funds, sovereign wealth funds, endowments, and pension funds can hold onto investments for the long-term. This is ideal for hard assets since it can take time to generate strong returns. With the scale and strong financial resources of institutional investors, they will continue to be a powerful source of demand.

---

[2]www.un.org/en/global-issues/population

- Supercycle: This describes the long-term growth in commodities. Examples of this include periods of 1906 to 1923, 1933 to 1953, and 1968 to 1982. Why have there been supercycles? A key reason is the long-term nature of hard assets. If prices increase, the supply will usually take a while to meet the demand. For example, suppose the price of copper is increasing and you want to capitalize on this. First, you will need to explore for copper deposits, and this will usually be in remote, dangerous areas. Then you will need to negotiate with a government to get the rights and permits for a mine. Once approved, you will hire people and purchase equipment for the mine. In other words, this process can take years to complete.

- China: The country is one of the biggest consumers of commodities. Note that it represents 30% of the demand for the global supply of copper.[3]

- Technology: The growth of new technologies is a major driver for commodities. An example is the smartphone, which includes a variety of valuable commodities like rare-earth minerals, and tungsten. Or look at EVs (Electric Vehicles). They need commodities like cobalt, lithium, and graphite. For example, lithium demand is forecasted to double or triple by 2030.[4]

---

[3] www.barrons.com/articles/commodities-investing-copper-corn-oil-what-to-know-51641609490?mod=hp_LEAD_1
[4] www2.deloitte.com/ca/en/pages/energy-and-resources/articles/commodities-of-the-future-predicting-tomorrows-disruptors.html

Note   For university endowments, Yale is a pioneer in investing in hard assets and alternative investments. The strategy was the mastermind of David Swensen. From 1985 to 2021, the value of the portfolio went from $1 billion to $31 billion.[5] Currently, only about 10% of the investments are in US stocks.

There are a myriad of advantages for investing in hard assets. For example, they usually have less correlation compared to stocks and bonds. This allows for more diversification for a portfolio.

To understand this, let's take an example. Suppose inflation starts to accelerate. This should mean that commodities will have higher prices. However, companies that rely on these will be squeezed. They may pass on some of the costs along to customers – but there are limits to this. The result is that there will often be pressure on profits, and this will weigh on the stock price.

Another benefit of hard assets is that they can be a hedge against inflation. A reason for this is that – as the currency loses value – investors will want more stable assets.

But some hard assets have ways to generate more income during inflationary periods. This is the case with commercial properties, which often have escalation clauses in rental agreements.

Note   J.P. Morgan did a study on energy futures and US inflation. The conclusion was that – since 2000 – there was a 76% correlation between the Bloomberg Commodity Index and the consumer price index, which is a key measure of inflation.[6]

---

[5] www.universityworldnews.com/post.php?story=20210514132514505
[6] www.barrons.com/articles/commodities-investing-copper-corn-oil-what-to-know-51641609490?mod=hp_LEAD_1

On the other hand, there are notable risks to investing in hard assets. Perhaps the biggest one is oversupply. This can result in plunges in the prices of commodities – and it can take a considerable amount of time for the supply to be absorbed.

Next, hard assets have the costs of storage and upkeep. They can be exacerbated when the market is oversupplied.

Interestingly enough, global warming can be another factor. Governments and companies are under pressure to find ways to reduce their carbon footprint. But this could ultimately mean lower demand for traditional energy sources like crude oil. Consider that mega energy companies like Exxon, Chevron, and BP have started to invest in transitioning to renewables.

Note   The next frontier for finding valuable commodities – like rare-earth minerals – is space. This is about mining asteroids, which are remnants of planets. The objects do not have enough mass for heat to impact the distribution of the elements. This means it is easier to mine them versus the earth. Governments are investing in missions for asteroid mining as well as companies like Planetary Resources, Asteroid Mining Corporation, or Trans Astronautica Corporation. Astrophysicist Neil deGrasse believes the first trillionaire will be a space miner.[7]

---

[7] www.bbvaopenmind.com/en/science/physics/asteroid-mining-a-new-space-race/

Real Estate

Real estate remains a great source of wealth creation. Just look at the Forbes 400 list. In 2021, there were 24 members on it who were real estate owners and developers. In all, the net worth was $122 billion.[8] At the top of the list was Donald Bren, who owns the Irvine Company. He controls over 126 million square feet of real estate in southern California. He also owns over 560 office buildings, such as the MetLife Building in Manhattan. Oh, and his portfolio includes 125 apartment complexes. His total net worth: $16.2 billion.

Keep in mind that there are many long-term trends that should help with the growth of real estate. Here's a look:

- Ecommerce and Logistics: According to eMarketer, ecommerce spending in the United States increased 17.9% in 2021 to $933.3 billion.[9] This represented 15.3% of total retail sales. By 2025, the spending on ecommerce is forecasted to reach $1.648 trillion. With this growth, there has been demand for warehouses and distribution centers. These are usually large but also located near major population centers. This allows for same-day shipping or even deliveries by the hour.[10]

---

[8] www.forbes.com/sites/giacomotognini/2021/10/05/the-richest-real-estate-billionaires-on-the-2021-forbes-400-list/?sh=35e8304f6324

[9] www.emarketer.com/content/us-ecommerce-forecast-2021

[10] www.wsj.com/articles/cbre-investment-to-buy-4-9-billion-in-warehouses-in-u-s-europe-11641295802?mod=hp_major_pos2#cxrecs_s

- Infrastructure: President Biden's $1.2 trillion infrastructure bill will be a strong catalyst for growth. This will facilitate investments in highways, bridges, EV charging stations, and airports. However, there are other areas of infrastructure that should continue to grow. Examples include fiber cables for internet access, wireless towers, and systems for renewable energy.

- Senior Living Facilities: The Covid-19 pandemic had a devastating impact on this industry. But by 2022, there were signs of improvement, especially as many residents got vaccinated. There was also the benefit of new treatments. Now, in terms of the long-term trends, they are certainly favorable for senior living centers. The Census Bureau forecasts a 36% increase in residents by 2030 because of the aging of the population.[11]

- Data Centers: The growth in data, cloud computing, mobile, and IoT (Internet-of-Things) are just some of the growth drivers for this market. So it should be no surprise that the data center category has seen lots of interest from some of the world's top investors. In 2021, there was a record $47.1 billion in acquisitions, up more than 3X in 2019.[12]

---

[11] www.wsj.com/articles/the-senior-living-stock-that-is-an-overlooked-reopening-play-11626087600

[12] www.wsj.com/articles/property-investors-swap-office-blocks-for-data-centers-11641818815

- Self-Storage: This got a big boost from the Covid-19 pandemic. After all, people needed to make more room for home offices. But there are secular trends at work as well. Perhaps the biggest is that Americans have a penchant to spend money on goods. But another factor is the continual changes in people's lives, whether that be marriages, divorces, going to college, or moving. The economics of self-storage are definitely favorable. The upkeep for the facilities is fairly minimal. The rental process is quick, which can take about 10 minutes. Interestingly enough, companies are looking at self-storage as an option. That is, it has become more affordable to store inventory.[13]

- Biotech: According to research from Global Market Insights, the biotechnology market is expected to reach $775 billion in the United States by 2025.[14] This means there will be a growing need for facilities. But of course, they will be specialized and custom built. As a result, landlords can charge higher rents. The tenants also have long-term contracts. In light of all this, biotech has been one of the hottest categories of the real estate market. One of the most active investors is the Blackstone Group.[15]

---

[13] www.wsj.com/articles/self-storage-is-the-pandemics-hot-property-11640132345
[14] www.biospace.com/article/global-biotechnology-market-4-pivotal-trends-expected-to-augment-the-industry-size-through-2025/
[15] www.wsj.com/articles/blackstone-raises-wager-on-life-sciences-with-3-5-billion-property-deal-11607950801?mod=article_inline

No doubt, there are areas of real estate that could struggle. For example, office buildings could see slower growth rates because of the move toward remote work and hybrid arrangements. This has also weighed on retail properties.

Investing in Real Estate

Investing directly in real estate can be lucrative. As seen on popular television shows on HGTV, you can buy beaten down homes and flip them for higher amounts. Or you can buy a duplex, office building, retail mall, and so on.

There are advantages to direct ownership in real estate. Often there is leverage involved in a transaction, which can magnify returns (then again, the opposite is true if the value of the real estate drops, as was the case during the financial crisis). There are also lucrative tax advantages. Here are some common ones:

- Deductions: You can take deductions for the operating expenses of the property. Examples include expenses for mortgage interest, property management fees, advertising, equipment, salaries, legal and accounting, and maintenance.

- 1031 Exchange: Suppose you want to buy a new property but will have to sell another one to finance the purchase. If the property you purchase is equal to or higher in value than the one you will sell, you will pay no taxes. This is an effective way to defer taxes on your real estate portfolio. In fact, there is no limit on how many times you can use a 1031 exchange.

- Qualified business income (QBI): This is a complex rule, but it allows you to take up to 20% of your deductions on your personal return.

- Depreciation: This means you can take a deduction for the wear and tear of an asset. For example, if you buy a rental property for $500,000 and the structure has a value of $350,000, then you can depreciate the $350,000 over a fixed period of years (its 27.5 years for residential properties and 39 years for commercial properties). In some cases, you may deduct a higher proportion in the early years.

Despite all this, the direct investment in real estate can be time-consuming and expensive. You also will need lots of startup capital and expertise. You may even have to personally guarantee loans. If the value of the real estate investment fails, your personal assets could be in jeopardy.

Yet there are easier ways to get exposure to real estate investments. A common approach is with a REIT (Real Estate Investment Trust). These are funds – which are usually publicly traded – that focus on certain real estate properties or investments.

Congress created REITs with legislation passed in 1960. This was a way to encourage more private investment in real estate. For the most part, the REIT proved to be quite successful, and many other countries would go on to adopt the structure.

A key is the tax advantages. If a REIT pays at least 90% of its income as dividends, there is no corporate tax. As a result, this type of security usually has a relatively higher yield.

Here are the different types of REITs:

- Equity REITS: These are the most common. They own or operate properties – like apartments or commercial real estate – that generate income.

- Mortgage REITs or mREITS: These invest in mortgage securities. The REIT generates income from interest and the return of principal.

- Non-Traded REITs: These are REITs that are registered with the SEC, but not traded on a stock exchange.

Until recently, non-traded REITs were not popular. They usually had high minimum investments and lacked transparency.

But firms like the Blackstone Group have revolutionized the non-traded REIT market. It has made it an effective way for retail investors to get access to investments that have been only available to institutions and very wealthy people.

The main offering from Blackstone is the BREIT (Blackstone Real Estate Income Trust).[16] The fund has about 1,600 properties and $66 billion in assets. About 87% of the properties are in residential, industrial, and net lease sectors. The occupancy rate is roughly 95%.[17] From 2019 to 2021, the average return was 15.2% (this includes the appreciation of the real estate and the yield).[18]

The Blackstone Group – which is the world's largest owner of real estate – does extensive research and takes a thematic approach to its investments. It also focuses on high-quality properties in attractive markets, such as where the population is growing.

The BREIT has a minimum investment of $2,500. However, you need to use the services of a financial advisor to make a purchase.

---

[16] www.breit.com/

[17] www.breit.com/wp-content/uploads/sites/4/2019/12/BREIT-Marketing-Presentation.pdf?v=1640041025

[18] www.wsj.com/articles/blackstone-property-fund-targeting-small-investors-passes-50-billion-11642510801

Crowdfunding

Crowdfunding allows for a large number of investors to pool their money to back direct investments in real estate. This is done through a website. Because of this, the minimum investment levels can be low, such as $100. This makes it possible to diversify your money across different properties.

Crowdfunding can be for any form of real estate, say for residential, office, retail, and so on. There will also be managers of the property, who will put the financing together, and manage the properties. Some of the crowdfunding sites will also have complex transactions, such as with 1031 exchanges.

The top sites include:

- RealtyMogul

- Fundrise

- YieldStreet

- CrowdStreet

While sites may vet their deals, you should still do your own homework and research. It's also important to note that these investments are risky. If the management team is not strong or the markets take a dive, you could lose considerable sums. Also, even if an investment does well, it could take a few years to get your money back.

Commodities

There are many commodities available to invest in. But here are the main categories:

- Agriculture: Corn, wheat, soybeans, cotton, sugar, cocoa, orange, juice, coffee, and oats

- Livestock: Live cattle, feeder cattle, pork bellies, and lean hogs

- Precious Metals: Gold, silver, and platinum

- Industrial Metals: Copper, palladium, aluminum, tin, nickel, zinc, lead, and cobalt

- Energy: Crude oil, unloaded gasoline, natural gas, coal, heating oil, uranium, ethanol, and electric power

You can buy commodities directly (this is known as investing in the spot market). But except for such items like gold or silver, this is usually not practical. After all, how would you buy uranium? What would you do if you bought crude oil?

Because of this, the most common way to invest in commodities is on the futures markets. This allows you to buy or sell a commodity at a future date for a fixed price. A future is a contract, and they are traded on exchanges like the CME Group. To make trades, you will set up a brokerage account.

For example, suppose you are interested in trading in the corn market. A contract on the CME is for 5,000 bushels and the price is $3 per bushel. You buy one futures contract for delivery in March. Even though the total value is $15,000 or $3 multiplied by 5,000 bushels, you do not put up this amount. You will instead use about 10% of it for your deposit. This is known as margin. If the value of corn drops, you will have to add more margin to your account. Or, if the price increases, you will have more equity in your account and can borrow against it.

There is something that's extremely important, though. When you want to close your position, you will need to make an opposite transaction. In our case, you would sell one futures contract. If the price is higher than $3 a bushel, you will have a profit and vice versa.

What if you did not close out the futures contract? Well, there would be delivery of 5,000 bushels to you!

When you sell a futures contract, this essentially means you are short selling the commodity. That is, you will make money on the transaction if the price of the underlying commodity falls.

When it comes to investing in commodities, perhaps the most important factor is the supply and demand. For example, if there is adverse weather, this could lower the yield for crops. The result could be a spike in the prices. Or if the weather is moderate, then there may be a bumper crop. And yes, prices may fall.

The price of a commodity can greatly impact the price of another. This is often the case with the price of energy. If it is higher, this will mean higher costs for operating tractors and other farm equipment.

Then there are long-term drivers for supply and demand. One case is the trend toward healthier foods. This has resulted in higher demand for commodities like soybeans, nuts, and avocados.

Note   On April 20, the futures contracts on West Texas Intermediate crude oil dropped a stunning 300%.[19] The price per barrel hit -$37. This was in response to the Covid-19 pandemic, as demand for oil plunged.

There are various ETFs that invest in commodities. However, the expenses can be high because of the need to manage complex futures contracts. Another issue is that indexes cannot provide good coverage of the myriad commodities. For example, they may leave out fast-growing ones like lithium.

---

[19] www.cnbc.com/2020/06/16/how-negative-oil-prices-revealed-the-dangers-of-futures-trading.html

Because of this, many investors will instead focus on actively managed ETFs. Some examples include Pimco CommodityRealReturn Strategy, Columbia Commodity Strategy, and BlackRock Commodity Strategies.

Gold

Back in 700 BC, gold coins started to emerge.[20] They would quickly become a key for monetary systems. But when paper currencies started to become popular, gold would still be important. Many nations would use it to back the value of the currency. This became known as the gold standard. This would instill more trust in paper-based money. There was also protection against inflation. If a nation started to print lots of paper currency, people could just convert it to gold.

However, by the 20th century, the gold standard would ultimately be abandoned. This was an attempt to make it easier for governments to spend more money to deal with recessions and depressions.

Despite all this, gold has remained popular with investors. It is considered a hedge against inflation. It is also something that is deemed to be a "safe haven." For instance, during the financial crisis of 2008, gold bullion jumped 26% while the S&P 500 dropped 54%.[21]

But gold is more than just an alternative to money. It has important economic uses, such as for jewelry, dentistry, medicine, clean energy, and industrial purposes.

---

[20] https://goldprice.com/project/the-history-of-gold/
[21] https://sprott.com/investment-strategies/physical-bullion-trusts/the-case-for-gold-in-crises/

Note   There are certainly notable skeptics of gold as an investment. Consider Warren Buffett. In 1998, he said, "(Gold) gets dug out of the ground in Africa, or someplace. Then we melt it down, dig another hole, bury it again and pay people to stand around guarding it. It has no utility. Anyone watching from Mars would be scratching their head."[22] But in 2020, he would actually spend $563 million in shares of Barrick Gold, which is a top producer of gold.[23] But he would sell his position a year later.

The world supply of gold is about 200,000 metric tons and has a value of over $11 trillion.[24] There are various ways you can invest in it. A common approach is to buy gold bars or coins from dealer websites. But you will either need to store it yourself or use a third-party. No doubt, you want to make sure it is secure, such as in a safe. You may even consider buying insurance.

Next, there are ETFs that have vaults of gold bars. The biggest one is SPDR Gold Shares, which has over $57 billion in assets. The expense ratio is a reasonable 0.40%.

You can also purchase ETFs that invest in gold futures or the shares of miners. Some examples include VanEck Gold Miners ETF, and VanEck Junior Gold Miners ETF.

[22] www.kitco.com/news/2021-02-18/Warren-Buffett-exits-GOLD-entirely.html

[23] www.kitco.com/news/2020-08-14/Warren-Buffett-buys-gold.html

[24] www.wsj.com/articles/how-to-invest-in-gold-11607378054

Artwork

It was a blockbuster year for art sales in 2021. Christie's International reported annual sales of $7.1 billion, which was the highest in its history. Rival Sotheby's also had a record year.[25] The sales reached $7.3 billion.

As expected, there was strong demand for the works of master artists. Note that Pablo Picasso's "Woman Seated Near a Window (Marie-Thérèse)" sold for $103.4 million (it was a portrait of his mistress). But there was also strong interest in emerging types of art, like NFTs.

The recent growth is nothing new, though. Art has been a reliable asset class for diversification. It also has a history of being a hedge against inflation. Then there is the impact of the rising wealth across the world.

A new generation of investors is making an impact. Millennial collectors have become influential buyers of artwork. In 2021, 35% of new bidders were first-timers and about a third of them were millennials.[26]

Note   From 2000 to 2021, the art asset class outperformed the S&P 500 and returned over 360%.[27]

Yet you do not have to be wealthy to invest in art. Over the past decade, there has emerged a variety of online sites that make it easier and more affordable to make purchases. Some examples include Yieldstreet and Masterworks.

---

[25] www.wsj.com/articles/christies-sells-7-1-billion-in-art-the-highest-in-five-years-11640020357#:~:text=Priciest%20Picasso%2C%20Record%2DBreaking%20Beeple,%247.1%20Billion%20in%20Art%20%2D%20WSJ
[26] www.wsj.com/articles/christies-sells-7-1-billion-in-art-the-highest-in-five-years-11640020357#:~:text=Priciest%20Picasso%2C%20Record%2DBreaking%20Beeple,%247.1%20Billion%20in%20Art%20%2D%20WSJ
[27] www.yieldstreet.com/investing-in-art/

The online portals provide an array of services, such as:

- Analysis using sophisticated databases to evaluate the return of artwork

- Negotiations for the purchase and sale of artwork

- Third-party appraisals

- Ownership authentication

- Storage and upkeep

- Insurance

- Regulatory filings

The minimum investment levels are reasonable, say at $5,000 to $10,000. Since the money is pooled among many investors, you can get a fractional ownership in high-quality artwork, and this is usually in the form of shares. There may even be a secondary market where you can sell them.

An online portal will hold onto the artwork for a period of time, say three to ten years. After this, it will look to sell it – hopefully at a nice profit. The online portal may charge ongoing management fees as well as a fee for the sale.

Conclusion

Hard assets are a way to diversify your portfolio and provide a hedge against inflation. There are also key drivers that should help generate positive long-term returns. They include factors like global growth, institutional interest, the impact of China, and the changes from new technologies.

The good news is that it is much easier to invest in hard assets. There are many ETFs and REITs to choose from. There are also crowdfunding sites for real estate and artwork. But in some cases, you might want to own the commodity directly, such as with gold.

In the next chapter, we'll take a look at asset allocation.

CHAPTER 8

Asset Allocation

Where to Put Your Money

> *I think that the first thing is you should have a strategic asset allocation mix that assumes that you don't know what the future is going to hold.*[1]
>
> —Ray Dalio, hedge fund manager

While at the University of Chicago in 1950, Harry Markowitz was searching for a dissertation topic. So one day, he was waiting for a meeting with a professor and overhead a conversation from a stockbroker. Markowitz wondered: Might the stock market be a good choice?

At the time, this was somewhat controversial. Many Americans still had distrust of the stock market because of the crash in 1929 and the Great Depression. The belief was that it was a place of manipulation by the wealthy.

But Markowitz went ahead anyway. It probably helped that he grew up in a moderately wealthy family. He also did not have any experience trading in the market.

---

[1] https://youberelentless.com/the-top-quotes-on-asset-allocation/

© Tom Taulli 2022
T. Taulli, *The Personal Finance Guide for Tech Professionals*,
https://doi.org/10.1007/978-1-4842-8242-7_8

By 1952, his research would pay off. He published a monumental paper called "Portfolio Selection" in the Journal of Finance. He looked at how to analyze risk – which he measured as volatility of securities prices – and return for constructing portfolios. At the heart of this was looking at assets related to each other. By doing this, an investor could better achieve diversification and higher risk-adjusted returns.

Markowitz's theory would become the basis of Modern Portfolio Theory. As a result, he would win the Nobel Prize for Economics for his work.

In this chapter, we'll take a look at one of the core ideas of Modern Portfolio Theory – that is, asset allocation. We'll cover the fundamental ideas and how you can pursue it for your own investments.

What Is Asset Allocation?

On its face, asset allocation is a fairly simple concept. It's about having a fixed percentage of assets in different types of investments. The most common one is the 60/40 allocation. This is where 60% of your portfolio is in stocks and the remaining is in bonds and cash. The 60/40 approach provides the potential long-term upside from equity growth but has downside protection with fixed-income securities.

But of course, this approach does not fit everyone's situation. If you are 90 years old, then you may not want as much risk in your portfolio. You may want something like a 30/70 allocation.

Or if you are in your 20s, you have many years to ride out the volatility in the markets. In this case, you might look at an allocation of 70/30 for your portfolio.

Financial planners have sophisticated software that can help come up with the allocation. Often this is based on answering a questionnaire, which takes into account your age, financial goals, and risk tolerance. The software will have the benefit of processing large amounts of market data. There will also be the use of Monte Carlo simulations. This is where the asset allocation is based on thousands of hypothetical market scenarios.

Then again, if you want to do the asset allocation on your own, there are a variety of free online apps. They often take less than ten minutes to fill out. The result will get a nice chart and useful recommendations.

Some free online apps to consider include the following:

- Vanguard: `https://investor.vanguard.com/calculator-tools/investor-questionnaire/`

- Smartasset.com: `https://smartasset.com/investing/asset-allocation-calculator#YN3vVUmwLp`

- Bankrate.com: `www.bankrate.com/calculators/retirement/asset-allocation.aspx`

Another option is to use a robo advisor. This is an app that will automate the process by using sophisticated algorithms and data analytics. It will connect to your investment assets from other accounts and have a questionnaire. From this, the robo advisor will build a portfolio, suggest different allocations, and may even provide tax optimizations. This process may take just a few minutes.

The investment minimums are low, say at $500. In terms of the fees, these are also reasonable. They typically range between 0.25% to 0.50% of the assets in your account. There are usually no transaction fees or commissions for trades.

The robo advisors typically use ETFs for the investment options. While there may not be fees for these, there will still be the underlying expense ratios.

Here are some of the top robo advisors:

- Sofi

- Wealthfront

- Betterment

- Acorns

- Schwab

- ETrade

Some robo advisors have financial advisors that can help with questions or complex planning. This can be via email, text, or video conference. But this will likely increase the cost of the service. For example, Schwab has a $300 upfront fee and monthly charge of $30. There is a minimum account requirement of $25,000.

However, a robo advisor may not necessarily offer access to alternative assets like hedge funds, private equity funds, crypto, and hard assets. This is why you might want to consider using the services of a qualified financial planner. They can provide a more customized asset allocation and financial plan.

While asset allocation is a proven strategy, it still has its flaws. Let's take a look:

- Risk Tolerance: Answering questionnaires can be more of an abstract experience. You may think you can handle higher risk. However, when you actually experience a brutal bear market, how will you feel then? It's common for investors to get extremely nervous and rashly sell their holdings. Often this is the worst time to do so.

- Correlation: Over the years, different assets have become more similar in terms of their movements. A big part of this is the speed of trading and the access to information. The rise of index funds may have also resulted in higher correlations. Because of this, when there are major drops in the market, the diversification may not necessarily provide much downside protection since all assets could fall.

Note   Volatility is generally the norm with the stock market. Since the S&P 500 was launched in 1957, every year there has been one 10%+ decline and more than three 5%+ drops.[2]

Rebalancing

As time goes by, there will likely be some major divergences in the asset classes for your portfolio. For example, you may have started with 60% in stocks and 40% in bonds but then the stock market stages a huge rally. Now the stocks represent 80% of your portfolio.

What to do? You may want to consider rebalancing. This means that you bring down the percentage to your original mix.

The frequency of the rebalancing is an important consideration. Some investors may do this every quarter, six months, a year, or longer.

Then what is best? It's a tough question. Some investors may wait longer. The reason is that they believe it's a good idea to "let your winners ride." After all, when a market is in the bull phase, this is usually not temporary. It could easily last a few years.

On the other hand, this is a form of market timing. It also means you are rethinking your willingness to take risks.

For the most part, asset allocation is not something that is a science. The key, though, is to have a diversified portfolio and exposure to a broad set of asset classes. Ultimately, this could mean having some rebalancing, but not necessarily back to the original percentage.

---

[2] www.barrons.com/articles/stock-market-volatility-investing-opportunities-51643420533?mod=hp_HERO

Yet, for some types of assets, you might want to have more frequent rebalancing. This is the case with volatile investments like crypto. They may surge 50% or more within a couple months. In this situation, it is probably a good idea to take some profits and redeploy them in other asset classes. Just as speculative investments can quickly soar, they can also quickly plunge.

Target-Date Funds

A target-date fund will allocate the portfolio across different asset classes. They are also based generally on the year you will retire. For example, you can have a target date fund for 2030, 2040, and so on. Over time, the target-date fund will change the asset allocation based on risk levels (this is known as the glidepath). So as you get closer to retirement, the investment strategy will be more conservative.

A target-date fund is certainly convenient. You get the benefit of a disciplined approach based on the insights of experienced money managers. They usually focus on index funds, which lowers the costs. Note that target-date funds are popular with 401(k)s and IRAs.

Regardless, there are issues with these funds. Perhaps the biggest is that they are a one-size-fits-all approach. But of course, each investor has their own goals and risk levels. There may also be life changes. If you lose your job, then you may want more conservative investments that provide income.

Note   Academics at the Massachusetts Institute of Technology and the University of Illinois analyzed target-date funds. The main conclusion was that the asset allocation mixes were too conservative.[3] The result is that investors likely lost out on potential long-term gains.

One trend is for financial planners to outsource the asset allocation to a money management firm. This is done by using a model portfolio fund, such as from BlackRock, Fidelity, or Schwab. This is often a good solution since it is based on sophisticated analysis and customized to the client's needs. There are also ways to provide for factors like ESG and taxes.

Emergency Fund

It's a good idea to have an emergency fund. This is cash you set aside for something like an unexpected bill or a layoff. The general rule is that you should have three to six months of living expenses saved. Although, if the job market is uncertain or you are a freelancer, then you may want this to be longer.

You want to have the money in an account that is easy to access. It could be a savings account. Or it could be a money market fund. This is essentially a mutual fund that is very liquid. The investments are in short-term and high-credit-rated bonds, often issued by the US government. The fund will pay interest, say on a monthly basis. But it is usually a low percentage because of the liquidity and safety of the account.

---

[3] www.wsj.com/articles/why-target-date-funds-might-be-inappropriate-for-most-investors-11641500579

You will buy a money market fund from a brokerage or mutual fund. But there are also money market accounts or MMAs, which are issued by banks. Because of this, they are backed by the FDIC or Federal Deposit Corporation. If the bank fails, the federal government will cover up to $250,000 per depositor.

Regardless, they both have similar features like check writing and electronic transfers. There are also no loads or exit fees. Something else: money market funds and MMAs have a NAV of $1 and this is supposed to not change. However, during the financial crisis, there was a money market fund – called the Reserve Primary Fund – that "broke the buck." In response to this, Congress set forth stricter regulations to prevent this from happening. That is, money market funds and MMAs can only invest in certain types of securities and have short term maturities.

Here are some of the categories of funds:

- Government Money Funds: This has a minimum of 99% of its assets in cash, government debt, and repurchase agreements.

- Prime Money Market Fund: These invest in higher risk securities like corporate bonds. As a result, this fund does not abide by the $1 NAV requirement.

- Tax-Exempt Money Fund: This holds investments in securities that are exempt from federal taxes. If the fund has municipal bonds, then the interest may be free from state taxes.

Hedging Your Portfolio

Bill Ackman is one of the world's top investors. He runs the Pershing Square hedge fund.

From 2020 to 2021, he pulled off two major bets on the markets. In February 2020, he realized the Covid-19 pandemic would be a global problem. But it would have been difficult for him to unload all his positions.

Instead, he hedged his holdings. This means he took short positions, which amounted to only about $27 million. But they paid off in a huge way. Within a few weeks, the positions were worth roughly $2.6 billion.[4]

As for the other bet, he made leveraged trades in stocks that would benefit from the improvement in the economy. Part of this was investing in companies like Hilton, Lowe's, and Burger King.

The bottom line: In 2020, the hedge fund posted a gain of 70%, and there was a 27% gain the following year.

Of course, Ackman used highly complex investments. But there are much easier ways to hedge your portfolio. As we saw in Chapter 4, you can invest in ETFs – like AdvisorShares Active Bear ETF and ProShares Short S&P 500 ETF – that short the market.

Having some short exposure is definitely worth considering. It does not have to be a big position. It could be a few percentage points of a portfolio. However, in volatile markets, it can help soften the downside.

Day Trading

From 2019 to 2021, there has been significant growth in day trading. This is where people's main activity is to invest their own portfolio, and this often means focusing on short-term gains.

---

[4] www.wsj.com/articles/bill-ackman-scored-on-pandemic-shutdown-and-bounceback-11643634004?mod=hp_lead_pos6

There have been waves of day trading, such as what happened during the 1990s. But they usually do not last long and are often powered by the frothiness in the markets. The reality is that it is extremely difficult to make money by timing investments.

Regulators are concerned about the current spike in speculative trading. It's not uncommon for the traders to use leverage, whether through the use of borrowing from their brokers (through a margin account) or using stock options. However, if the markets fall, these positions can generate substantial losses.

A key concern of regulators is a practice called "payment for order flow." This is where a brokerage firm will get fees on allocated transactions to market makers, which are Wall Street firms that handle transactions in certain stocks. They do this by making profits on the differences with the bid and ask prices on the securities.

The order flow payments are considerably higher than for regular stock. Regulators are worried that brokerage firms are financially incentivized to encourage risky trades. The order flow payments may also mean that investors take on higher costs for the trades.

Something else to consider: Financial apps – like Robinhood – use gamification to encourage more trading. Again, this can increase risky behavior.

At this writing, the regulators have not enacted any rules. But this could happen within the next few years – and this could have a major impact on the markets.

Note   Elon Musk is the richest person in the world, with a net worth of $235 billion. So you would think his financial matters are very complex? Not according to him. In an interview, he noted his financials are not a "deep mystery" and that he could do his own taxes in a few hours.[5] He also mentioned that he does not use any offshore accounts or tax shelters.

Conclusion

Asset allocation can help to improve the risk-adjusted return on your portfolio. But this is based on factors like your goals, age, and tolerance for risk.

There are various ways to use asset allocation. You can use an online calculator or the assistance of a financial advisor. There are also robo advisors that automate the process. Then there are target funds that are based on your age.

Besides this, it is recommended to have a certain amount of your assets in cash. This is for an emergency fund.

You might also want to consider hedging your portfolio. Even a small amount in a short ETF can provide some downside protection.

In the next chapter, we'll take a look at benefits.

---

[5] www.msn.com/en-us/money/companies/elon-musk-my-wealth-isn-t-some-deep-mystery-my-taxes-are-super-simple/ar-AAS447Z?ocid=msedgntp

CHAPTER 9

Benefits

Retirement Plans and Health Insurance

Retirement is not in my vocabulary. They aren't going to get rid of me that way.

—Betty White[1]

An effective tool to recruit prospective employees is to offer attractive benefits packages and perks. Consider Block, which is a top provider of online payments (the company was formerly called Square). Some of the benefits include free meals for breakfast, lunch, and dinner; parental leave for mothers and fathers; and onsite services for acupuncture, massage, and meditation.[2]

Of course, these programs are far from cheap. Benefits often represent a large part of a person's salary. According to data from the US Bureau of Labor, they are roughly 31% of total compensation.[3]

In this chapter, we'll take a look at the main benefits, which include those for retirement, and health insurance.

---

[1] www.brainyquote.com/topics/retirement-quotes
[2] https://tech.co/hr-software/best-companies-employee-benefits-perks
[3] www.embroker.com/blog/cost-of-employee-benefits/

© Tom Taulli 2022
T. Taulli, *The Personal Finance Guide for Tech Professionals*,
https://doi.org/10.1007/978-1-4842-8242-7_9

401(k)

For a tech company, the 401(k) is the most common retirement account. There are annual contribution limits, which adjust based on inflation. For 2022, the maximum is $20,500 and it is $27,000 for those aged 50 or older. Your employer will make the contributions by using automatic payroll deductions.

A 401(k) comes with lucrative tax benefits. First of all, your contributions are deductible from your income. For example, if you contribute $20,000 and your total tax rate is 30%, then you will save $6,000.

Next, the earnings in your 401(k) account – such as capital gains, dividends, and interest – are tax deferred. This means that you do not pay taxes until you withdraw your money. The idea is that – by the time you retire – you'll be subject to a lower tax rate.

Note   Some companies allow you to exceed the 401(k) contribution limits. However, the additional contributions are not tax deductible.

Your employer will have a set of investments options. They will often cover a variety of funds, such as for stocks, bonds, and foreign investments. It's also common to have target-date funds (see more about these in Chapter 8). Keep in mind that the funds are usually actively managed and are not based on indexes.

There could be the option to invest your money in your employer's stock. There may even be a deferred annuity, which is a vehicle that provides a fixed amount of income for the rest of your life.

If you withdraw money before reaching 59 ½, you will not only have to pay taxes on the amount but also a 10% penalty. But the IRS does provide exceptions to the penalty:

- Down payment on your first home

- Qualified educational expenses

- Up to $5,000 for expenses related to birth or adoption (this is according to the SECURE Act of 2019)

- Hardships, which are defined as having an "immediate and heavy financial needs."

You can also have penalty-free distributions if you use rule 72t (this refers to the IRS code). You do this by making Substantially Equal Periodic Payments (SEPPs). The IRS provides three options for this.

A 401(k) will also have a penalty for those who do not withdraw funds once a person reaches age 72 1/2. This is known as a required minimum distribution (RMD). This starts at about 4% of the total amount in your account and increases over time. Your bank, brokerage, or financial services company will disclose what you need to withdraw.

What if you do not comply with the RMD? The penalty is a stiff 50%.

Employer Matches

Some employers will match part or all of your contributions. This is free money! In other words, one of the smartest things you can do is to make sure you contribute enough money to get the match.

The employer will usually have a maximum limit, which is a percentage of your salary. This may be 4% or so.

Then what about the $20,500 or $27,000 contribution limits? These apply to you, not your employer. Your employer has other contribution limits.

An employer may also use vesting restrictions, which will encourage retention. This could be a four your schedule, in which you get ownership of 25% of the match after each year at the company. Then there is cliff vesting. In our example, this means that you get 100% of the match after four years. But keep in mind that vesting only applies to matches, not the contributions you make.

401(k) Loans

You are allowed to borrow from your 401(k). This avoids having to pay taxes or the 10% penalty.

Based on your employer's policies, the amount you can borrow can be as much as 50% of the value of the account for a maximum of $50,000. This is for a 12-month period.

You will pay interest on this loan and need to repay the loan amount, usually by five years. Note that the interest goes back into your account, and you can invest the money.

However, if you leave your job or are terminated, you will likely have to repay your loan. If you cannot do so, the amount you withdraw will be subject to taxes and the 10% penalty. A silver lining is that a default does not appear on your credit rating.

Roth 401(k)

So far in this chapter, we have been focusing on the traditional 401(k). But your employer may offer another flavor – the Roth 401(k).

Yet it generally is not as popular. Some people may not even know that their employer offers it.

Despite this, a Roth 410(k) can be a good option and there are many similarities with the traditional 401(k), such as:

- Earnings in your account grow tax free.

- The annual contribution limits are the same as a traditional 401(k).

- There is the potential for employer matching.

- You can invest in various investment options, say mutual funds or your employer's stock.

- You can take a loan against the value of the account (limits depend on your employer's policies).

So, what are the differences? The main one is that you cannot deduct your contributions from your income. But there are some things that make up for this. For example, you can withdraw money from the account tax-free and without having to pay a 10% penalty. This is if you

- Held the account for five years and

- You are 59 ½ or you died or have a major disability.

If you do not meet these requirements, your initial contributions into the account will be free from tax. Instead, you will pay the tax on the earnings generated in your account.

This is done by prorating the amounts. Here's an example: Suppose the total value of your account is $20,000. This includes $16,000 from contributions (80% of the total) and $4,000 in earnings from your investments (20% of your total). If you withdraw $5,000, then 80% of this or $4,000 will be considered to be from your contributions and not taxable. The remaining amount, or $1,000, will be earnings and subject to taxes and perhaps a penalty.

One reason to use a Roth 401(k) is that if you expect your tax rate – when you retire – to be at least as high as it is now. Next, there are no income restrictions on the contribution limits. This is a major benefit for higher-income people.

Now the Roth 401(k) is subject to RMDs. However, you can avoid this by rolling over the account into a Roth IRA.

Note   RMDs do not apply to a 401(k) if you are still on the payroll past the age of 70 ½.

During the year, you can contribute to both a traditional and Roth 401(k). But they cannot be simultaneous. One approach is to make contributions to one during the first half of the year, and the second one for the rest. To do this, you will need to talk to your HR department or plan administrator.

No Retirement Plan

If you work for an early-stage startup, you may not have access to a traditional 401(k) or Roth 401(k). But there are other retirement options.

You can have an Individual Retirement Account (IRA), which you can set up with a bank, brokerage firm, or other financial services company. Like a 401(k), your contributions are deductible and the earnings in the account accumulate tax free. If you make withdrawals before age 59 ½, you will be subject to taxes and a 10% penalty. But after this, there will be no penalty. Moreover, the RMD rules apply.

For 2022, you can contribute up to $6,000 in an IRA. There is an additional $1,000 for those who are 50 and older.

Then there is the spousal IRA. This is where you can set up an IRA for a spouse who has little or no income. The contribution limits are the same as for a regular IRA. But you need to file a joint tax return.

However, if your spouse works and has an employer that offers a retirement plan, then your tax-free contributions may be reduced based on the family income level.

Next, there is the Roth IRA. Like a Roth 401(k), the contributions are not deductible, but the earnings are generally tax free (see earlier in the chapter for the rules). The contribution limits are the same as for the traditional IRA. But they are reduced based on your modified adjusted income (MAGI). You can contribute the maximum if you are single, and your MAGI is less than $129,000 or if you are married and filing jointly and your MAGI is less than $204,000. For income above these limits, the contribution amount is gradually phased out.

IRA Investments

A nice benefit of an IRA is that you can allocate the funds across a wide assortment of investments, whether ETFs, mutual funds, or stocks. You can even invest in the following:

- Commodities like gold and silver

- Real estate properties

- Private equity interests

But be careful. There are certain types of investments to avoid, like variable annuities. After all, they already benefit from tax deferral of the earnings.

Note   You cannot put collectibles, gems, antiques, rare books, or art in an IRA.

While an IRA is a good way to save for your retirement, the contribution limits are a big drawback when compared to traditional and Roth 401(k)s. But a strategy is to ask your employer for you to become a contractor (although, you need to factor in the need for getting your own health insurance, which we will cover later in this chapter).

Why do this? You can set up these retirement accounts:

- Simplified Employee Pension Plan (SEP) IRA: This is essentially an IRA that allows contributions of 25% of your compensation or $61,000, whichever is less. There are no catch-up contributions for those 50 or older. A SEP IRA also has RMDs.

175

- Solo 401(k): This is essentially a traditional or Roth 401(k) for one person. For 2022, the contribution limit was $61,000 and there was a $6,500 catchup contribution if you are 50 or older.

- Pension: This is a retirement account that guarantees a certain benefit when you retire. However, this can be expensive to set up and manage.

Finally, you can set up a Health Savings Account, which can actually be a useful vehicle for saving for retirement. We'll cover this type of account later in the chapter.

Note Managing your own retirement account takes discipline. It is not always easy to keep writing checks. This is why a good approach is to set up an automatic investment program with your bank account. This will make it similar to a paycheck deduction system for an employer-based 401(k).

401(k) Rollovers

If you lose or leave your job, then you need to make a decision about your 401(k). You can keep it with your employer if the account has at least $5,000 in investments. A common reason for this is if you are 55 or older. This means you can make penalty-free withdrawals from the 401(k).

Another advantage is if you have stock that has appreciated significantly. The amount you contributed is taxed as ordinary rates and the gains are taxed at capital gains rates, which will likely be lower. For example, suppose you bought your company stock for $10,000 and included it in your 401(k). After three years, you leave the firm, and the stock is now worth $50,000. Assume your ordinary tax rate is 35% and your capital gains rate is 20%. In this situation, the taxes on the $10,000 will be $3,500 and $8,000 for the gains – for a total of $11,500. However, if you transferred your account to an IRA, the taxes would have been $17,500.

There are some downsides to maintaining your account with your employer. There may be limits on when you can take money, and the staff may be less responsive because you are a former employee. You also cannot make any new contributions.

Another option is to move your account to your new employer's 401(k) or an IRA or Roth IRA (there are no limits on the amount). There are two ways for this:

- Direct Rollover: This is the easiest option. You fill out a form and the plan administrator will handle the transfer.

- Indirect Rollover: This is where the plan administrator sends you a check for the amount in the account. You will then have to transfer this to the new account. If this is not done within 60 days, you will owe taxes and a 10% penalty on the amount (if you are younger than 59 ½). Another issue: Your former employer will withhold 20% of the amount for taxes. While you will get this back, you will need to file a tax return. This means that – in the meantime – you will only be able to invest 80% of your own funds.

Regardless of the type of rollover, your employer will usually liquidate your account and issue a check. After this, you will set up your portfolio.

So, what account should you rollover into? There's no clear-cut answer. In one sense, a 401(k) is better since you can borrow against it. But an IRA or Roth IRA certainly have their advantages as well. You will have many more investment options available. The fees may be lower too.

The Super IRA

Before becoming a Governor, Senator, and a Presidential candidate, Mitt Romney was a successful partner at Bain Capital, a private equity firm. From 1984 to 1999, he was able to accumulate anywhere from $21 million to $102 million in his IRA, according to campaign disclosures.[4]

But this was not a one off. Just look at Peter Thiel. He is one of Silicon Valley's most successful founders and investors. He co-founded breakout companies like PayPal and Palantir. He was also the first outside investor in Facebook. Other notable investments included SpaceX, Asana, Lyft, and Airbnb.

As for his IRA, it has exceeded $5 billion.

OK then, how did Romney and Thiel amass huge sums in their IRAs? In the case of Romney, it's not clear. Although, one theory is that he allocated limited partner interests of Bain Capital in his IRA when the valuations were extremely low.

As for Thiel, he used a Roth IRA to buy 1.7 million shares of PayPal in 1999 for $1,700.[5] When the company sold to eBay in 2002 for $1.5 billion, he reinvested his gains in other startups – all tax free.

These examples show how retirement vehicles can be an extremely effective way of creating wealth. But there are risks too. Tax advantages can be easily changed.

For IRAs, Congress has been exploring ways to make it more difficult to accumulate large sums in the accounts. After all, these accounts were meant for middle class people to save for their retirements – not for billionaires.

---

[4] www.investmentnews.com/cohan-the-mystery-of-mitt-romneys-magic-ira-45612

[5] www.marketwatch.com/story/how-peter-thiel-turned-2-000-in-a-roth-ira-into-5-000-000-000-11624551401

Health Insurance

The US healthcare system is the largest in the world. According to CMS.gov, the amount spent on it came to $4.1 trillion, or $12,530 per person in 2020.[6] It's nearly 20% of the gross domestic product.

While the US healthcare system has many positives – especially the vibrant innovation of biotech and pharma companies as well as many highly skilled physicians and healthcare workers – there are many downsides. Besides the high costs, there are many complexities. The billing systems can be mind-numbingly difficult. Then there is the jargon.

But to get the most of your healthcare benefits, you need to understand the basics. So let's first look at some of the key terms for the ways you pay for your services:

- Premium: The amount you pay – each month – for the policy.

- Deductible: The amount you pay out-of-pocket for your medical expenses before the insurance company covers the costs of your medical care.

- Copayment: This is a fixed amount for each doctor visit, which can range from $15 to $50 or so. This does not apply to your deductible. Even after you cover your deductible, you still must pay the copayment

- Coinsurance: This is the percentage you pay for certain services after you meet the deductible. For example, you may have to pay 20% for a hospital visit.

---

[6]www.cms.gov/Research-Statistics-Data-and-Systems/Statistics-Trends-and-Reports/NationalHealthExpendData/NationalHealthAccountsHistorical#:~:text=U.S.%20health%20care%20spending%20grew,spending%20accounted%20for%2019.7%20percent.

- Maximum out of pocket: This is the maximum you pay for your policy for the year. After this, the insurance will cover all your costs. But in the following year, the health insurance policy starts again from zero.

There are a variety of ways you can receive your services. These involve the use of plan types and include a provider network. This is essentially a list of doctors, hospitals, facilities, and other healthcare professionals. If you use someone outside of the provider network, you may have to pay part or all of the bill.

Here are the main plan types:

- HMO (Health Maintenance Organization): This type of plan will only pay for services from the provider network. An HMO typically has lower costs because of more stringent policies. You also will need to select a primary provider and get referrals for specialists.

- PPO (Preferred Provider Organization): You have more discretion in selecting your healthcare providers, and you do not need a referral for specialists. Although, the network may be relatively small. The premiums are usually higher for PPOs, and you will likely get some coverage for help outside the network.

- POS (Point-of-Service) Plan: This has features of both an HMO and PPO. You get the discretion of selecting your healthcare providers, but there is also less paperwork when you see those outside of the network. The PPO will provide you with a primary doctor.

- EPO (Exclusive Provider Organization): Like a PPO, you have more options when selecting your healthcare providers, and there is no need for a referral for a specialist. But there is no coverage for getting care outside the network.

Regardless of the plan, they all provide necessary services for emergencies that involve providers outside the network. Yet there are occasions when you may get hit with a huge bill. Unfortunately, this often means having to deal with a complex bureaucracy, and it can take time to resolve the matters.

For the most part, it's recommended to use in-network providers. This should help keep your healthcare at lower levels. It's always smart to ask for discounts as well.

You should read your policy and see what is covered. This can avoid having to pay potentially large bills. Keep in mind that health plans often change.

For example, if you go on vacation in another country, your plan may not provide coverage. You may want to get a travel policy.

In some cases, you may have a minor ailment. For this, the cheaper alternative may be to go to a local clinic at CVS, Walgreens, Walmart, or Target.

Your plan may even have some interesting perks. Examples include weight-loss programs, massage therapy, and gym memberships.

By law, a health insurance plan must provide preventive services for free. Some examples include cancer screenings, immunizations, and mammograms.

Since you have to pay for your healthcare costs before you hit the limit on your deductible, it is worth looking at ways to economize. There are a myriad of apps and services that can help out. One is GoodRx. This app allows you to get significant discounts on prescriptions and OTC (over the counter) medications (if purchased at a pharmacy), which can be over 80%.

Then there is ClearHealthCosts.com. This service provides the cost breakdowns for healthcare procedures in various cities. Interestingly enough, you might find that paying out-of-pocket may be cheaper than using insurance, since there will be a copayment or coinsurance.

Flexible Spending Accounts (FSAs)

An employer may offer a flexible spending account (FSA) as a supplement for the health plan. You will select it during the open enrollment season for the company.

For 2022, you can contribute a maximum of $2,850 and this is deductible. You can use this money for qualified medical expenses – tax free. Your employer will usually provide you with a debit card for the transactions.

Typical qualified expenses include:

- Prescription medications

- Wheelchair

- X-rays

- Annual exams

- Dental procedures

- Fertility treatments

- Surgery

- Lab fees

- Pregnancy tests

- Physical therapy

As for what is not covered, these usually include procedures purely for cosmetic purposes. However, before you make a purchase with an FSA, check your plan to make sure that it is covered. You also need to maintain documentation of your expenses, such as with bills and invoices. In some cases, you may have to get a letter from your physician for certain treatments. This is called a letter of medical necessity. Keep in mind that –

if you make an unqualified expenditure – it will be subject to taxes and a 20% penalty. The penalty applies until your reach 65, which is when you become eligible for Medicare.

FSAs are usually based on the principle of "use it or lose it." That is, by the end of the year, any unspent funds will revert to the employer. Because of this, you should try to estimate your annual costs before contributing to your FSA.

Some employers may allow you to carry over unspent funds to the following year. The limit is $570 for 2022. Or an employer may give you a grace period of the first 2.5 months of the following year to spend the money in your FSA.

Next, there is the dependent care FSA. This is for expenditures for children under 14 years of age or for your spouse or relatives who cannot care for themselves. Some common qualified expenditures include babysitting, nanny, day care, nursery school, preschool, and eldercare. The maximum contribution is $5,000 for a married couple filing jointly and $2,500 for a single person.

Health Savings Accounts (HSAs)

An employer may offer a health savings account (HSAs). This is if you have a high-deductible health plan. This means that – if you are single – the deductible on the policy cannot be lower than $1,400. The amount is $2,800 for a family plan.

For 2022, a single person can contribute a maximum of $3,650 for an HSA account and $7,300 for a family. These amounts are tax deductible. If you are over age 55, there is an additional $1,000 for the annual contribution.

You can pay for qualified medical expenses with an HSA, and they are tax free (see the prior section for examples of these).

A nice feature of an HSA is that you can carryover all unspent contributions to the following year. In fact, you can invest the funds in mutual funds and interest-earning accounts. This means you can use an HSA as a way to help fund your retirement.

If you withdraw money, you will owe taxes on the amount and pay a 20% penalty. But like an FSA, the penalty goes away after you reach 65. Interestingly enough, the HSA does not have RMDs.

If you leave your job, you keep your HSA. You can rollover the account into another one, such as with a brokerage firm or bank.

COBRA (Consolidated Omnibus Budget Reconciliation Act)

If you leave your employer, you can continue your health insurance. This is according to COBRA (Consolidated Omnibus Budget Reconciliation Act). You can maintain your coverage from 18 to 36 months. But you will need to pay 100% of the premiums.

Yet COBRA is a good option. You do not want any gaps in your health insurance coverage. You can then spend time looking for another job – and get a new plan – or you can buy a healthcare plan from the Affordable Care Act exchange.

Affordable Care Act (ACA)

The Affordable Care Act (ACA) – or Obamacare – is an option if you work for a small company that does not offer health insurance or you are self-employed. This allows you and your family to get coverage even if there are preexisting conditions, like cancer, diabetes, or even a pregnancy.

The enrollment is usually from November 1 to the end of December. But some states may extend this to January 31. If you miss this, you may meet the requirements for Special Enrollment. This means you can enroll any time if you have a life event, such as the loss of a job, you move out of the coverage area, or you get married.

All ACA plans must provide ten essential health benefits. They include:

- Emergency services

- Hospitalization

- Laboratory services

- Mental health and substance use disorder services

- Outpatient care

- Pediatric services

- Pregnancy, maternity, and newborn services

- Prescription drugs

- Preventive care, wellness services, and chronic disease management

- Rehabilitative and habilitative services and devices

- Note: All children will get dental coverage.

To sign up for ACA health insurance, you can enroll online at Healthcare.gov or your state's marketplace. You can also call at 800-318-2596. For free, you can get the help of a navigator.

For an ACA policy, you will fill out a form that requests information about your family, income, address and so on. You will then shop around for a policy, which include Bronze, Silver, Gold, and Platinum. They have different premiums, copays, and maximum costs. There are also varying levels of services, drug coverage, and networks.

If you have significant medical needs, you may first want to look at the total costs of the coverage – which is the annual deductible plus the maximum out-of-pocket costs – as an initial filter. You can then research the providers and services. You can also see the types of drugs that are available, which is provided on the formulary on the profile page for the insurance company.

ACA policies have subsidies, which reduce the costs of the insurance. This applies to those households with income of 100% to 400% of the federal poverty level.

The ACA handles the tax subsidies through the use of tax credits. You have two options. First, you can estimate your income, and then the monthly premium will be reduced. Or, you can get the tax credit when you file your tax return.

If you take the first option, there is a potential problem – that is, if your income increases. This could mean that you will need to reduce your refund or even have to pay a higher tax. This is why you might want to be conservative with your estimate of your annual income.

Conclusion

Benefits are certainly complex and confusing. Even experts have problems understanding them. But it is a good idea to read through the materials. You can also get the help of an insurance agent or financial planner.

As we've seen in this chapter, there are some big gotchas with benefits. You definitely do not want to get hit with a huge bill.

You should also take advantage of the employer matches. This is an easy way to boost your investments for your retirement.

For the next chapter, we'll take a look at employee stock options and other equity compensation.

CHAPTER 10

Equity Compensation

Employee Stock Options, Restricted Stock, and ESPPs

> *If you are a CEO/Director of a public company, or investment fund, NOW is the time to re-evaluate your comp and reward structures and look at bottom up rather than top-down reward structures & give equity to everyone...*
>
> —Mark Cuban, entrepreneur and investor[1]

In late 2021, Elon Musk polled his Twitter followers the following: "Much is made lately of unrealized gains being a means of tax avoidance, so I propose selling 10% of my Tesla stock. Do you support this?"[2]

About 60% voted yes.

Musk would go on to aggressively sell his shares. But this was really about paying taxes on employee stock options that he received in 2012 from Tesla.

---

[1] www.businessinsider.com/mark-cuban-says-ceos-should-give-all-employees-stock-options-2020-6

[2] https://twitter.com/elonmusk/status/1457064697782489088?ref_src=twsrc%5Etfw%7Ctwcamp%5Etweetembed%7Ctwterm%5E1457066048944066565%7Ctwgr%5E%7Ctwcon%5Es2_&ref_url=https%3A%2F%2Fwww.theverge.com%2F2021%2F11%2F7%2F22768364%2Felon-musk-poll-twitter-tesla-10-percent-billionaires-capital-gains-tax

© Tom Taulli 2022
T. Taulli, *The Personal Finance Guide for Tech Professionals*,
https://doi.org/10.1007/978-1-4842-8242-7_10

To this end, he exercised more than 22.8 million shares for a value of over $16 billion.[3] Musk indicated that this would allow him to pay $11 billion in taxes.

True, this is a very unusual situation. Then again, when it comes to employee stock options, the taxes can be a major factor – and be very complex. In this chapter, we'll take a look at what you need to know, in terms of the types of equity compensation and strategies.

The Basics of Employee Stock Options

A stock option is a contract between you and a company. This allows you the opportunity to buy a fixed number of shares at a specified price.

But the option will likely have vesting. This means you need to work for the company a certain period of time to get ownership.

To understand this, let's take an example. Let's say you get a job at an exciting startup, which is Cool Corp. The company grants you an option to purchase 20,000 shares for $1 each, which is the exercise price. You usually have ten years to exercise the option (as we saw in our example with Musk).

When you receive a stock option grant, there is generally no taxes owed. Rather, the taxes come when you exercise the option and sell the stock. We'll cover this later in the chapter.

Of course, there will be some paperwork when you get a stock option grant. Here are common documents:

- Option Agreement: This is a contract that shows the terms of the options. They include the number of shares, exercise price, vesting, termination clauses, and so on.

---

[3] www.wsj.com/articles/elon-musk-exercises-final-batch-of-tesla-stock-options-behind-ceos-recent-share-dealings-11640748564#:~:text=Mr., the%20transactions%20began%20last%20month.

- Stock Option Plan: This is a document that sets forth
  the rules and procedures for all of the option grants.
  The company's board of directors must approve the
  stock option plan.

Note   What happens if you do not exercise your option after ten years? The option contract is no longer valid and there is no recourse. Because of this, if there is any value before expiration, you should exercise it.

In terms of vesting, a company will have a fixed period of time. It's common for this to be four or five years. In our example, if the vesting is for four years, then at the end of each year, 25% of the option will vest or 5,000 shares (20,000 multiplied by 25%).

Suppose a year passes, and you get your first vesting. The stock price has gone to $4, and you have a gain of $15,000. This is $4 minus the $1 exercise price – which is then multiplied by 5,000 shares. Your option is considered to be in-the-money.

But this is a "paper" profit. You only make money when you exercise and sell the shares. To do this, you will need to fill out a form, which can be online or a physical document. There may also be a need for various legal signoffs, such as from the company's counsel. This is especially the case if you work at a private company (later in this chapter, we'll look more at the process of how to sell shares that are not publicly traded).

There are different ways to pay for the shares:

- Cash: You write a check and get possession of the
  shares. You then deposit them in a brokerage account.
  You can then sell or hold onto them.

- Cashless Exercise: A bank or brokerage firm will make a temporary loan, which lasts a few minutes. This will make it possible to purchase and then immediately sell the shares. The difference in the amounts will go to you, after subtracting fees and commissions.

- Sell-to-Cover: This is similar to a cashless exercise – except, with a sell-to-cover transaction. That is, only the number of shares needed to pay for the exercise price will be sold. In this case, you will then own the remaining shares.

OK, in our example, let's suppose that Cool Corp.'s stock price drops to 50 cents a share. There is then no value to your option and it would not make sense to exercise it. Your option is considered to be "under water." This happens when the stock price falls below the exercise price.

Note   You cannot put your employee stock options in an IRA. This is forbidden by law.

Now that we have a backgrounder on employee stock options, the next step is to look at the different types: nonqualified options and incentive stock options.

Nonqualified Stock Options

A nonqualified stock option (NQSO) is an employee stock option that does not provide favorable tax treatment. This is the most common in Silicon Valley and for publicly traded companies. A NQSO can be issued to both employees and contractors like board members and consultants.

Here's an example. Suppose you are an engineer at Cool Corp. and the company grants you a NQSO for 1,000 shares and the exercise price is $25.

When the first 250 shares vest after a year, the stock price for Cool Corp. is at $35 per share. This means your gain is $250, as seen below:

Proceeds from the Exercise (250 shares X current stock price of $35)
$8,750
Minus
Purchase Amount of the Exercise (250 shares X the exercise price of $25)
$6,250
= $2,500

The gain is also known as the bargain element. According to the IRS, it is treated as ordinary income, which means it is similar to your salary or bonus. This means your taxes will be for the same tax bracket. Here's a look at this for both a single and a married taxpayer:

Single

Tax Rate	Taxable income	Taxes
10%	$0 to $10,275	10% of the income
12%	$10,276 to $41,775	$1,027.50 plus 12% of the amount over $10,275
22%	$41,776 to $89,075	$4,807.50 plus 22% of the amount over $41,775
24%	$89,076 to $170,050	$15,213.50 plus 24% of the amount over $89,075
32%	$170,051 to $215,950	$34,647.50 plus 32% of the amount over $170,050
35%	$215,951 to $539,900	$49,335.50 plus 35% of the amount over $215,950
37%	$539,901 or more	$162,718 plus 37% of the amount over $539,900

Married Filed Joint

Tax rate	Taxable income	Taxes
10%	$0 to $20,550	10% of taxable income
12%	$20,551 to $83,550	$2,055 plus 12% of the amount over $20,550
22%	$83,551 to $178,150	$9,615 plus 22% of the amount over $83,550
24%	$178,151 to $340,100	$30,427 plus 24% of the amount over $178,150
32%	$340,101 to $431,900	$69,295 plus 32% of the amount over $340,100
35%	$431,901 to $647,850	$98,671 plus 35% of the amount over $431,900
37%	$647,851 or more	$174,253.50 plus 37% of the amount over $647,850

As you can see, the tax rates increase as your income rises. This is because the United States has a progressive system. For example, if you are married and file a joint return, then the first $20,550 will be taxed at 10%, the income from $20,551 to $83,550 is taxed at 12% and so on.

Let's take an example of how to calculate your taxes. Suppose you and your spouse have a combined income of $220,000. First, you will go to the second column in the chart and select the one where $220,000 fits. This is for the 24% bracket. Next, go to the second column and then use the tax for $30,427. This is the tax for all the prior rates up to $178,150. Then you will add the tax of 24% on anything above this, which is $41,850 ($220,000 taxable income minus $178,150) multiplied by 24% or $10,044. This provides a total tax of $30,427 plus $10,044 or $40,471.

Let's return to our example with Cool Corp. Since you are an employee of the company, it will use withholding for the $2,500. This means it will take a portion out of your paycheck for income taxes, state taxes, Social Security, and Medicare.

When Cool Corp. sends you a W-2 the following year (usually in late January), it will have the following:

- Wages, tips, other compensation (Box 1): This will include the bargain element.

- Federal income tax withholding (Box 2): This will likely be a flat rate of 25% (if you are lucky enough to make over $1 million, then the rate is 39.6%).

- Social Security wages (Box 3): This will include the amount of your bargain element. But the maximum that can be taxed for Social Security is $147,000 (for 2022).

- Social Security tax withheld (Box 4): The tax rate is 6.2%.

- Medicare wages and tips (Box 5): This will include the amount of your bargain element. And unlike Social Security, all your income is subject to the Medicare tax.

- Medicare tax withheld (Box 6): The tax rate is 1.45%, which increases to 2.35% (for single people with taxable income over $200,000 and for married couples whose taxable income is more than $250,000).

- See Instructions for box 12 (Box 12a): The letter "V" will be in the first column and "NSQO spread" will be in the second column.

- State (Box 15–20): In these boxes, your employer will withhold state and local taxes.

In all, you may owe a considerable amount in taxes. This is especially the case if the bargain element is in the six figures, which is not uncommon for tech companies.

Note that the amounts withheld may be too low and this could mean having to owe more taxes when you file your 1040 return. You could also owe penalties and interest. To avoid this, you use estimated payments. You will file Form 1040-ES with the IRS, which you can do via mail or online. You will need to do this if you owe more than $1,000 in federal taxes for the year. Online systems like TurboTax or HRBlock.com can handle the calculations and process.

Let's continue with our NSQO example. You now own 250 shares of Cool Corp. You then wait a few months and sell them. What happens? It depends on the price of the stock.

If it is higher than the price of the date of the exercise, you will have a short-term capital gain, and this will be taxed at your ordinary rates. However, if you sold the shares more than a year later, there would be a long-term capital gain and the tax rate would be lower. For the most part, a key strategy is to try to find opportunities for long-term capital gains.

The tax is based on the amount realized – which is what you sold the shares for – minus the cost basis. The cost basis is what you paid for the shares.

But there is a hitch. True, when you exercised the NSQO, you paid $6,250 for the shares. You also paid taxes on the $2,500 bargain element.

So, what is your cost basis? It's actually $8,759, which is the $6,250 plus $2,500.

Keep in mind that some taxpayers miss this. And this means paying a higher tax.

Let's continue with our example. Suppose you sell your 250 shares at a price of $50. Your amount realized is $12,750. In this case, you will owe taxes on a capital gain of $4,000 or $12,750 minus the cost basis for $8,750.

Now if you sold the 250 shares at a loss, you can offset this against other capital gains. However, if after doing this you still have losses, you can take up to $3,000 on your return. Anything else you can carry forward to future tax years.

In terms of reporting these transactions, you will receive a 1099-B form from your brokerage firm. You will then use this to report you gains and losses on IRS Form 8949 and Schedule D for your 1040 tax return.

Using Stock to Exercise Nonqualified Stock Options

You may be able to use stock to exercise an NSQO. Suppose that you already own 100 shares of Cool Corp., for a total value of $2,500. You can use 40 of these shares for the exercise of the NSQO. This means the total number of Cool Corp. shares will come to 160. This includes the 100 shares you already own minus 40 shares for the exercise and plus 100 shares you get from the exercise. Now you will still need to come up with cash to pay for the withholding, if you are an employee.

So why do this kind of transaction? Well, there are two key reasons. First of all, you may not necessarily want to come up with the cash for the exercise.

Next, there are tax considerations to take into account. For example, the exchange of the shares you own for the new ones is actually a tax-free transaction. The new shares have the same basis and holding period as the old shares.

Then, the additional shares you acquired from the exercise will have a holding period that starts at the time of the exercise and the cost basis will be the compensation income recognized.

Incentive Stock Options (ISOs)

With incentive stock options, you have the potential to get long-term capital gains treatment. But this does not come for free. You will also be subject to the Alternative Minimum Tax (AMT), which can be complicated and result in a higher tax bill.

195

There are certain requirements for an ISO, which include the following:

- An ISO may only be granted to an employee.

- The option plan must be approved by shareholders.

- The ISO cannot have an exercise price below the current stock price.

- The option must not last longer than ten years.

If you are not sure if your option is an ISO, then check with your HR department or representative.

This type of option also has the so-called "$100,000 Rule." This means that only up to $100,000 worth of an exercisable option may be deemed an ISO each year. Anything above this is a nonqualified option.

Let's take an example. You receive an option for 20,000 shares of Cool Corp. – with an exercise price of $15 – that vest over 4 years. This does not violate the $100,000 rule since, every year, the amount of vested stock is $75,000 or 5,000 shares per year multiplied by the $15 exercise price.

But then suppose your employer makes another grant for 4,000 shares, with an exercise price of $30. Each year, the total vested amount will be $105,000 or $75,000 plus $1,000 multiplied by $30 exercise price. In this situation, the $100,000 of your options will be treated as an ISO and the remaining $5,000 will be considered a nonqualified option.

There is an easy way to avoid having an ISO be subject to AMT. This is when you exercise the option and sell all the shares in the same year. This is known as a disqualifying disposition.

It can also be triggered by events other than the sale of the shares, including the following:

- Some types of hedging activities, which use special investment structures – like short selling or the use of put options – to lock-in a gain.

- Any gift, except for estate purposes or to a spouse, such as in the event of a divorce.

- Transactions for Transfer to a Uniform Transfers to Minors Act accounts or irrevocable trusts.

However, the following are not deemed to be dispositions:

- Borrowing money against your shares. This is often done with a margin account with your brokerage firm.

- Transfer because of a bankruptcy.

- Transfer to a revocable trust.

ISOs and AMT

Taxes can get quite complex with ISOs. Even experienced tax professionals have challenges with this part of the tax code. The main reason is how AMT works. So in this section, we'll take a look at some of the main scenarios.

But first, let's get an overview of AMT. It is a tax system that Congress legislated in the late 1960s. The goal was to prevent wealthy individuals from paying little or no taxes. This is where the "minimum" in AMT comes from. Essentially, Congress wanted to make sure that every taxpayer paid their fair share.

AMT is actually a separate tax system (hence the word "alternative"), and this certainly adds to the difficulties. And yes, there are many critics of AMT. The Tax Policy Center has called it "the epitome of pointless complexity."[4]

Unfortunately, this is spot-on. However, if you have ISOs, then you need to understand AMT. If not, you can get into lots of trouble.

---

[4] https://taxfoundation.org/taxpayers-subject-alternative-minimum-tax/

So, when does the AMT apply? This is not easy to answer. There are various rules on this. Basically, to truly know if the AMT applies, you will need to complete returns for both the federal tax system and AMT.

Regardless, there are certain factors that may potentially trigger the tax. They include the use of state and local state tax deductions, property taxes, the amount of interest on a second mortgage and, of course, the exercise of ISOs.

The AMT involves a multi-step process, which is done by filling out Form 6251. For the first step, you take your adjusted gross income (AGI) and then make certain adjustments or tax preferences, such as disallowing various deductions but also including income items like the gains from the exercise of an ISO. After this, you will get an amount called your Alternative Minimum Taxable Income or AMTI. You will subtract this by an exemption amount. For 2022, it is $75,900 if you are single and $118,100 if you are married and file jointly. But this amount phases out based on your AMTI. It comes to 25 cents per dollar earned when AMTI hits $539,900 for single filers and $1,079,800 for those who are married and file jointly.

Next, you will multiply the net amount of the AMTI by the AMT rate, which is either 26% or 28%. If you have an AMT foreign tax credit, you subtract it from the tax you owe.

Now let's see how much you may pay. For example, let's say you owe $45,000 in federal tax and your AMT amount is $40,000. In this case, you actually have no AMT.

But let's say in the following year you exercise an ISO and generate substantial income. Because of this, your federal tax is $125,000 but the AMT is $150,000. According to the IRS, you must pay $125,000 in federal tax and $25,000 in AMT (which is the total AMT minus the federal tax).

OK then, why is AMT a problem if the maximum rate is 28% when the maximum for the regular tax system is a much higher 37%? Some of the reasons include the phaseout of the exemption as well as the inclusion of the income from the exercise of the ISO.

So, when it comes to AMT, it is important to be diligent and to do your research. Or, if things get too complex, then it is a good idea to seek out advice from a tax professional. The fee for the service should be well worth it.

Next, let's take a look at some of the scenarios for ISOs. Suppose you get an ISO grant for 5,000 shares from Cool Corp. and the exercise price is $25. After a year, you exercise 1,000 shares while the stock price $60. Your bargain element is $35,000, which is $60,000 minus the $25,000 for the purchase price.

You hold onto the shares for the rest of the year. In this case, you will not report the $60,000 for federal tax purposes. You also do not have to pay Social Security or Medicare taxes. Your W-2 will also not disclose the bargain element as income.

However, the $60,000 bargain element will be an adjustment for AMT. Consider that this may not necessarily mean you have to pay this tax. Again, you will only need to do this if the overall AMT amount is higher than the federal tax, which could be based on various other factors than your stock options.

With our example, suppose you want to get treatment for a capital gain. This is done by having a qualifying disposition. The rule is as follows:

- You sell the shares at least one year after you exercised your ISO.

- You did this at least two years after they were granted.

- You continue to be an employee of the company.

In our Cool Corp. example, the $60,000 would be treated as a long-term capital gain, so long as you meet the above requirements. But this type of a transaction can be risky. For example, suppose you exercise the option, and you paid a substantial amount of AMT. But when holding onto the stock for a year after the exercise, the price plunges. Unfortunately, you would have paid taxes on a "phantom gain." That is, you paid taxes on the AMT even though you did not receive any cash.

You might be able to recapture some or all of this. The reason is that the amount of the AMT that exceeds the regular federal tax could become a tax credit (to calculate this, you use IRS Form 8801). You can use this to reduce future federal tax liabilities. But it may take a while to get the full benefit. To make sure you maintain it, you will need to keep filing Form 8801 and Form 6251. All in all, this is a complex area of the tax code and it's usually a good idea to get the help of an expert.

Note   In January following the year of your ISO exercises, your employer will send you a Form 3921. This will provide details of the transactions and be helpful for filing your tax return.

Restricted Stock

When a company grants you actual shares, they are referred to as restricted stock. There are two types: restricted stock units (RSUs) and restricted stock awards (RSAs).

Let's first take a look at RSUs. With these, you will get access to the shares when you meet certain requirements. The most common is that you have worked for the company for a specific period of time.

Then what are the other conditions that might apply? Well, a company may require that the company hit a sales level or a number of customers.

Before you meet the restriction on the RSUs, you do not own any of the shares. This means that you will not receive any dividends. These will only come after you get ownership. Although, a company may have a policy to pay a cash amount to you anyway.

As for taxes on RSUs, you do not owe anything for the grant. It's only when the shares vest that you will need to report ordinary income, which is the fair market value of the stock (you can subtract the amount paid for the shares, if this applies). Your employer will disclose this amount on your W-2.

You may owe more tax when you sell the shares – that is, if the stock price is higher. If this is done less than a year from the vesting, it will be a short-term capital gain.

OK, now let's take a look at RSAs. Sometimes they are called a stock grant or restricted stock. But for our purposes, we'll refer to them as RSAs.

Then what is the difference with the RSU? Well, with an RSA, you get the shares upfront. However, if you do not meet the requirements, you will forfeit them. For both RSUs and RSAs, the most typical condition is that you work for the company for a period of time.

Even though you get a stock grant with an RSA, the physical shares will likely remain with a third-party, such as an escrow agent. The main reason is that this provides a better way for the company to initiate a forfeiture. However, since you are still the owner of the shares, you will get any dividend payments.

Regarding taxes on RSAs, the rules are the same as for RSUs. You do not pay taxes on the grant. But you do so on the vesting for the fair market value of the stock.

Something else you should know is the Section 83(b) election. This is for RSAs or stock grants that allow for an early exercise.

Keep in mind that this is a very important part of the tax code when it comes to equity compensation. Also, this is usually for early-stage startups. All in all, it can mean big tax savings.

For example, suppose you get an RSU for 100,000 shares at 5 cents each. Then the startup takes off and when the first 25,000 shares vest, the stock price is at $1. In this case, the whole $25,000 is subject to your ordinary tax rate, which could be as high as 37%.

But had you filed a Section 83(b), then the situation would have been much different. In this case, you would owe ordinary income taxes on the $5,000 value of the shares at the time of the grant, or 100,000 shares multiplied by 5 cents each. Then any gain above this would be treated as a capital gain. If you hold onto it for over a year, then the maximum tax rate would be 20%.

Now, when it comes to a section 83(b), there are strict rules. First, you need to write a letter to the IRS about the transaction. This is usually less than a page. Then you need to send it to the IRS within 30 days of the grant. There are no exceptions.

Employee Stock Purchase Plans (ESPPs)

Employee Stock Purchase Plans (ESPPs) are generally for companies that are traded on an exchange, like NASDAQ or the New York Stock Exchange. They are actually a nice perk for employees. It allows for the purchase of company stock for up to a 15% discount. This is done through after-tax income and a payroll deduction. This can be a good way to build an equity stake in your employer.

Even though you get a discount, the IRS does not treat this as a taxable gain at the time of the purchase. This is so long as the ESPP is a qualified plan. Make sure to check this with your HR department.

All employees are usually allowed to participate in an ESPP. But if you have more than a 5% stake, then you cannot.

There are timing rules, though. For example, you can only enroll in an ESPP during certain parts of the year. Also, you will usually sign up through a brokerage account that is approved by your employer.

An ESPP program will have requirements on amounts for the contribution. It's common, though, for this to be at least 1% of your compensation or up to 15%. However, in any given year, the purchases cannot exceed $25,000.

What about when can you sell your shares? In general, you can do this any time. Yet if you want to maintain the favorable taxes – such as for the 15% discount – then the sale should be one year after the purchase and two years after the grant. If so, the gains will be taxed at long-term capital gains rates.

Preferred Stock and Equity Compensation

In Chapter 1, we looked at preferred stock. This was in terms of publicly traded companies. But keep in mind that venture capitalists will often receive preferred stock for their investments and there are usually more preferences and benefits. After all, these startups are high risk.

Here are some of the main characteristics of preferred stock for VCs:

- Liquidation Preference: In the event of liquidation or acquisition, the investor gets paid before the common shareholders. The investor may also negotiate liquidation preferences that are higher than the amount invested. For example, a 2X preference means that the investor will get twice the investment.

- Pro Rata Rights: The investor has the option to invest in follow-on rounds so as to maintain the current ownership percentage of the equity.

- Anti-Dilution: This means that some or all early investors will be able to maintain their existing ownership percentages. The company will issue additional shares to them. This is often triggered based on if the next round of capital is at a lower valuation. No doubt, this can greatly reduce the equity of the founders and employees.

For those who work at startups, it's certainly important to understand the investment terms. Even if a company is acquired, you may ultimately wind up with worthless options or other equity.

An example is Good Technology. This mobile security startup sold to BlackBerry for $425 million in 2015.[5] On the surface, it seemed like a good deal for employees. But because Good Technology raised substantial capital at robust valuations, there was little left for the employees. Their options were worth 44 cents a share while the venture capitalists' holdings were at $3 a share. Even worse, some employees even lost money because they had to pay taxes on inflated gains (one person's tax bill exceeded $150,000).

SPACs (Special Purpose Acquisition Companies)

You may work for a company that is a SPAC (Special Purpose Acquisition Company). This means that it went public in a different approach than a traditional IPO. Although, the common stock you receive is the same – and you can receive any type of equity compensation that's been mentioned in this chapter.

While the SPAC structure has been around since the early 1990s, it has gained in popularity since the emergence of the COVID-19 pandemic. The main reason is that it is easier in terms of the paperwork, due diligence, and regulations.

Here's how a SPAC works. There will be a sponsor, which includes a group of people who are usually experienced in business (say as CEOs or senior executives). They will then create a shell company that has no operations and retain a 20% equity stake in it. The sponsor will use this as a way to focus on a certain industry or market opportunity.

---

[5] www.nytimes.com/2015/12/27/technology/when-a-unicorn-start-up-stumbles-its-employees-get-hurt.html

The SPAC will then raise capital on the NYSE or NASDAQ. A large amount of the equity will usually be sold at $10 a share and then there will be a warrant attached to the offering. This is similar to an option, in which the holders of the shares can buy extra stock. The strike price of the warrant is often at $11.50 a share.

After this, the managers will seek out an acquisition candidate. They also have two years to take this action. If there is no deal, then the SPAC will need to return the funds to the shareholders.

For example, suppose Cool Corp. is a SPAC and it agrees to merge with ABC Corp. The shell will be renamed as ABC Corp. (by regulation, at least 80% of the proceeds of the public offering must be used for the deal). As a result, ABC Corp. is now publicly traded – but did not have to do this with the traditional IPO approach.

If the stock price of the SPAC increases, then the warrant can provide a nice additional return. Moreover, there is a redemption right, in which investors can agree to get their money back if they do not agree with the acquisition.

As for the disadvantages, there can be undue pressure on the managers to get a deal done. This may ultimately mean buying a company that is not a good long-term prospect.

There has also been more regulatory scrutiny of SPACs. There are concerns that the managers may not be doing enough due diligence or that the disclosures are not sufficient.

Liquidity Services

There are a variety of online platforms that help you sell your privately held shares. Some examples include EquityZen, Nasdaq Private Market, CartaX, and Forge Global.

These platforms have become very popular over the years. One reason is that many startups have waited to go public. Yet many employees still want to find ways to cash in their equity holdings, such as to diversify their assets or make a purchase (say for a home or car).

To use a liquidity service, here's a common process:

- Sign Up: You will register for an online account, and this may include a mutual NDA (non-disclosure agreement). This is to make sure that your shareholder agreement and company information remain confidential. The liquidity service platform will determine if your company is suitable for a transaction, such as in terms of market value and revenues. If so, you will upload various documents, like your option and shareholder agreements.

- Demand: The platform will see if there is enough interest for your equity. Note that they will have a pool of investors. But some companies will have auctions or tender offers for large amounts of stock. In this case, you can submit some or all of your shares. The buyers are often institutional investors like VCs.

- Agreement: If there is interest in your shares, the liquidity platform will enter into an agreement with you. The company will handle the paperwork and process the funds.

- Due Diligence: The liquidity service will review the shareholder documents to make sure you own the securities.

- Complete the Transaction: The liquidity platform will reach out to the company and work to complete the sale. This will involve a legal process with the company's counsel. After this, the proceeds will be transferred to your account.

The fees for such a transaction? It is usually a percentage of the amount sold – say 5% or so. The transaction process can also take one to two months.

For some platforms, there may be private loans. This is to allow for the exercise of the options. Given the high valuations of startups, many employees simply do not have enough available cash to make a transaction.

Negotiating Equity Grants

When you get an option grant, you should negotiate the terms. You could wind up with much more value from the equity.

True, when you get a grant, it may seem like a lot of shares. This is especially the case with an early-stage startup. For example, the option grant could be something like 20,000 or 50,000 or more shares. And yes, even if there is a $1 gain, this can mean a lot of money.

But do not be too focused on the absolute number of shares. Basically, you want to know another important number: how many shares of the company's stock have been issued. For example, if a company has 500 million shares outstanding, then your 20,000-option grant would represent a very small percentage of the equity of the company. In other words, ask the company for how many shares are outstanding. If the grant pales in comparison, then you can use this as a way to bump up your number.

Now, if this is not applicable, you should still negotiate on the number of shares anyway.

Something else: When you negotiate for more shares, you should also bring up that you will be taking on risk. Let's face it, a company's stock can be volatile or go out of favor. You are also likely taking a lower salary in exchange for your options. Bottom line: As much as possible, fight for more shares!

As time goes by and you get promoted and show your value to the company, then talk about another option grant. There is no reason why you can't have multiple ones.

Vesting is another critical area for negotiation. You want to get the value of your options as soon as possible. To this end, you can ask for a vesting schedule of three years or even two years. You should also request monthly vesting.

Finally, look to get accelerated vesting for your options. This means that all the shares are vested on an event, such as the acquisition of the company or an IPO.

Concentration Risk

Concentration risk means that you own an asset that represents a large percentage of your total assets – say over 20%. If the asset plunges in value, you would suffer a major loss. It could be a significant setback in achieving your financial goals.

In the tech world, concentration risk is actually common. A seemingly invincible company can quickly fall apart. Just look at what happened to BlackBerry and Yahoo!

Yet the temptation is to hold onto the options or stock too long. But when a tech company stumbles hard, it's very tough for a comeback.

This is why it is a good idea to consider selling your position when there is concentration risk. What's more, you should allocate the funds to holdings that are non-tech.

Another strategy for reducing concentration risk is to donate part of your stock to a charity. This can reduce your taxes and provide estate planning benefits. There are a variety of trusts and investment vehicles that can help with this, such as a donor-advised fund, private foundation, and a Charitable Remainder Trust.

You may also set up a collar on your stock position, which is a sophisticated hedging strategy. This is what Marc Cuban used in 1999. He sold his startup, Broadcast.com, to Yahoo! and his stock was worth about $1.4 billion. He setup a collar, which capped his potential gains $205 a share and provided for a floor of $85 a share.[6] Not long after, the dotcoms imploded, and Cuban was able to preserve about 90% of his wealth.

For executives, it can be difficult to deal with concentrated positions. One reason is that there is often a negative perception if they unload their stock. Wall Street may see this as a sign of a lack of confidence in the prospects of the company.

To help deal with this, there is the 10b5-1 plan. An executive can set this up to allow for periodic sales of the shares.

But there can be no change of the amounts. An executive also cannot setup a 10b5-1 plan when they have access to nonpublic material information. Often this means that it should be after the latest earnings report or a major announcement.

Borrowing Against Your Equity

It's known as the "buy, borrow, die" strategy. This is where you borrow against your equity holdings to pay for your ongoing living expenses. Assuming your equity holdings are large enough, you may be able to do

---

[6] https://markets.businessinsider.com/news/stocks/how-mark-cuban-saved-billions-yahoo-windfall-dot-com-crash-2020-6-1029303375#:~:text=Cuban%20worked%20with%20Goldman%20Sachs,Insider's%20homepage%20for%20more%20stories.

this without ever having to pay back the loan. You also may not have to pay taxes, unless you have enough assets to be subject to the estate tax.

This strategy is not new. But it has traditionally been mostly for the mega wealthy. However, as Wall Street has looked to grow, it has offered lending options to more and more clients.

The loans are lines of credit that are called securities-based loans. Such arrangements usually have little paperwork because of the use of stock as collateral. As for clients, they can borrow up to a certain amount – say to 50% of the overall value. The interest rates are typically competitive as well.

With a securities-based loan, you will have a check book or debit card that you can use for your purchases. It's all very simple and convenient.

Note   Securities-based loans have become quite popular with tech startup founders. A key reason is that it allows them to maintain control of their companies.

But there is a risk. If the stock price plunges, you will likely need to put up more collateral for your loan. And if you do not do so – or do not have enough assets – you will be forced to sell your stock. This often comes at the worst time. It could mean having a huge reduction in your equity holdings.

Conclusion

In this chapter, we have covered the main types of equity compensation, such as incentive stock options, nonqualified stock options, restricted stock, and ESPPs. We have also looked at preferred stock – for startups – and SPAC structures.

Ultimately, the equity can result in substantial gains in wealth. But you need to be aware of the tax consequences. If you have ISOs, then you may be subject to AMT. For the most part, you will probably need the help of a tax expert.

You can also use strategies to borrow against your holdings. While this has its advantages, it could also mean being exposed to substantial risks if the markets come under pressure.

As for the next chapter, we'll take a look at estate planning.

CHAPTER 11

Estate Planning

Providing for Your Loved Ones

Estate planning is an important and everlasting gift you can give your family. And setting up a smooth inheritance isn't as hard as you might think.[1]

—Suze Orman, finance author

Frank Slootman is one of the top CEOs in Silicon Valley. In 2003, he took the helm of Data Domain, which was a struggling storage startup. But he quickly transformed the company and growth surged. In 2007, he took the company public, and it was eventually sold to EMC.

After this, Slootman became the CEO of ServiceNow, a pioneer in the SaaS IT help desk market. He again made significant changes to the company. By 2012, he took ServiceNow public[2] and the value of the stock would eventually hit $109 billion.

---

[1] www.brainyquote.com/quotes/suze_orman_604382

[2] www.wsj.com/articles/snowflake-ceo-slootman-scores-ipo-hat-trick-with-big-bet-on-data-11600383892

© Tom Taulli 2022
T. Taulli, *The Personal Finance Guide for Tech Professionals*,
https://doi.org/10.1007/978-1-4842-8242-7_11

We would then go into semi-retirement. But this did not last long. In 2019, he became the CEO of Snowflake, a fast-growing online database provider. But he was able to accelerate the ramp even further and pulled off an IPO in September 2020. It was the largest software deal in history, as the company raised $3.4 billion.[3]

Needless to say, Slootman has accumulated substantial amounts of wealth. By 2022, Forbes.com estimated his fortune at $2.2 billion.

But Slootman has also been smart with his estate planning. He not only wants to provide for his family but also various charities. To this end, Slootman has established a trust.[4]

Granted, estate planning is something that people often avoid. No one wants to think about their death, right? Of course not. But despite this, estate planning is too important to ignore.

In this chapter, we'll look at the fundamentals and the different strategies.

Why Estate Planning?

By his mid-20s, Tony Hsieh was already a multimillionaire. During the 1990s, he sold his Internet startup, LinkExchange, to Microsoft for $265 million. He would then go on to found online shoe retailer Zappos. At first, the startup would struggle, but Hsieh found ways to ramp the growth. In 2009, he sold the company to Amazon for $1.2 billion.

Unfortunately, Hsieh's life would ultimately come to a tragic end. In late 2020, he died in a fire at his home in Connecticut. He was only 46 years old.

---

[3] www.cnn.com/2020/09/16/investing/snowflake-ipo/index.html
[4] www.sec.gov/Archives/edgar/data/1640147/000162828020013010/snowflakes-1.htm

Estimates of his wealth were over $800 million.[5] Yet Hsieh did not leave a will. As a result, there were a myriad of lawsuits. The resolution of his estate could eventually take many years.

This terrible incident shows the importance of estate planning. Without legal documents – like a will or trust – there is likely to be higher expenses as well as a longer process to resolve matters. This can actually reduce the value of the estate.

Here are some important benefits of estate planning, such as:

- You can provide instructions about how to handle your medical preferences. For example, if you are incapacitated, you can designate someone to make decisions on your behalf. Or you can specify how you want end-of-life care.

- You can name those who you trust to take care of your children.

- You can use legal structures to help reduce the potential tax burden.

- You can effectively gift assets, such as to your loved ones or favorite charities.

- With a trust, you can maintain privacy of your financial assets.

If anything, estate planning can mean less stress and problems for your family when you die. If not, the government will make the decisions – and they may not necessarily be what you intended.

---

[5] www.wsj.com/articles/zappos-founder-tony-hsiehs-friends-family-feud-over-his-500-million-estate-11639918803?mod=hp_lead_pos10

Will

A will is a legal document that allows you to distribute your assets to your heirs. You can also specify guardians for your minor children.

Each state has rules about the validity of a will. Usually, you will need several witnesses to be present and attest to your signing and dating of the document.

In the will, you will designate an executor. This is the person who will carry out your wishes. This can certainly be a major undertaking. So, make sure to talk to the person who you want to become the executor. If you have a complex estate, you may name an advisor to help. Or you can even have a bank or trust company manage the will.

When you die, your will goes through a judicial process called probate (assuming the value of the estate meets a certain level, according to your state law). This is where your will is validated. Depending on the estate, the process can take over a year and be expensive. This is why you might want to consider naming beneficiaries for certain assets and setting up a trust (we'll cover these topics later in this chapter).

After probate is completed, your will is filed with the court. This means the document will be publicly available. This is why we know about the estate plans of famous people.

Note   David Packard, the co-founder of Hewlett-Packard, died in 1996. In his will, he left a large portion of his $6.6 billion fortune to the David and Lucile Packard Foundation.[6] The organization currently provides support for causes like climate change, affordable healthcare, and STEM education.

---

[6]www.livingtrustnetwork.com/estate-planning-center/last-will-and-testament/wills-of-the-rich-and-famous/last-will-and-testament-of-david-packard.html

Regardless if you are diligent with estate planning, your will may not account for all your assets. For this situation, you can have a "pour-over will." This means that these assets will transfer to your trust.

Healthcare Documents

When it comes to healthcare, there are two main types of legal documents. First of all, there is the advance health-care directive. This is for your end-of-life wishes, such as for whether to continue life-sustaining measures (an example is to not use a respirator). You should provide the advance health-care directive to your family but also your doctors.

Next, there is the durable power of attorney. This is where you name someone to make financial or health decisions on your behalf when you are incapacitated. For example, they can pay your bills, sign legal documents, and so on.

No doubt, you should spend time on who you select for this role. Such a person will have lots of power.

Beneficiaries

A simple technique for estate planning is assigning beneficiaries for assets like bank accounts, brokerage accounts, 401(k)s, and insurance policies. This means that – on your death – the assets will transfer directly to the persons you name. There will be no probate.

You should also set forth contingent beneficiaries. This is for if the primary ones are no longer alive. If not, the assets will actually windup in your estate and will be subject to probate.

When you fill out the form for your beneficiaries, you will write their name, date of birth, the relationship to you, and the contact information. You may even be able to divide the assets among different beneficiaries.

What about your employee stock options and equity? The stock plan will indicate if you can name beneficiaries. Ask your HR representative for information about this.

Trusts

A trust is a common legal structure for estate planning. It means that a trustee will hold assets on behalf of a beneficiary or beneficiaries.

If properly set up, a trust can avoid probate. There are also potential tax advantages – this is, if you establish an irrevocable trust. With this, you will no longer have access to your assets. The transfer will be final.

Here are some other benefits of trusts:

- Privacy: Your trust does not become part of the public record.

- Control: There is much flexibility with trusts. For example, you can distribute assets to your heirs while you are alive. Or you can place conditions on the assets, such as an heir needs to finish college to get a certain amount of money.

- Asset Protection: A trust can provide protection against creditors.

There are many types of trusts. But the most common is the living trust or revocable trust. This means you retain control of your assets while you are alive. While this means you do not get tax benefits, there are certainly other important advantages. At any time, you can change the trust – say to add assets or take them out – or terminate it. A living trust is also generally affordable to establish.

Estate Taxes

The estate tax applies to those who have substantial amounts of assets. For 2022, the IRS requirement is that they must exceed $12,060,000 for an individual and $24,120,000 for a couple (these amounts exclude the debts of the estate). Of course, very few people pay the tax. In 2019, there were only 2,570 that did so, and the total amount owed was $13.2 billion.[7] The largest amount of the assets were in publicly traded stock.

By January 1, 2026, the estate tax will revert back to the levels of 2017. This will be $5,490,000 for an individual and $10,980,000 for a couple.

Keep in mind that some states have estate and inheritance taxes. They also may have much lower minimum asset requirements.

In other words, it is worth evaluating the use of trusts to help reduce the taxes. There are other strategies, such as gifting. This takes assets out of your estate.

Note   Determining the value of an estate can be challenging. This is especially the case if there is private stock, real estate, or other private interests. The estate may need to hire valuation experts. The valuation of the estate also must be either for at the time of death or six months later.

You and your spouse can each give up to $15,000 in gifts – each year – to family, friends, or charitable organizations. The recipient usually does not owe any taxes and there is no need to report the gift to the IRS (the exception is if the gift came from outside the United States).

---

[7] www.cnbc.com/2021/09/29/heres-how-many-people-pay-the-estate-tax-.html

If a gift exceeds the $15,000 annual limit, you will need to report this on a gift tax return or Form 709. This will lower the amount you can exempt from your estate tax threshold.

While gifting assets is a good strategy, there are drawbacks. For example, you may not want to have your children to have access to large sums of money. In this situation, you can set up an irrevocable trust and have your children as beneficiaries. You can then place restrictions on access to the money. You might allow access for when they reach a certain age or if they meet a milestone, like attending college.

There is an exception to the $15,000 annual limit. You can make unlimited payments to a medical or educational institution for others. This is so long as this is for qualified expenses, such as medical bills or tuition.

When you gift an asset like stocks or bonds, the recipient will get your cost basis. This can mean significant tax consequences if there is a sale. For example, suppose you gift 100 shares in Cool Corp. to your daughter and your cost basis is $1. But the current stock price is $20. If your daughter sells Cool Corp., the gain that is subject to tax will be $1,900 (this is $20 multiplied by 100 minus $1 multiplied by 100).

However, if the 100 shares are distributed when you die, there will likely be "stepped up basis." This is the current value of the stock. In our example, this means that the cost basis is $2,000 and no tax would be owed.

Note   Can you gift stock options or restricted stock? For most plans, this is not allowed.

Another common strategy is to donate appreciated stock to charities. By doing this, you will avoid capital gains tax. This also means the impact of the donation is higher. Besides having no tax, there is the potential for continued capital gains for the charity. Finally, you will be eligible for a deduction for the donation. This is up to 30% of your adjusted gross income.

Then, does it make sense to donate stock that is at a loss? The answer is no. It would actually be better to sell your stock – and get the capital loss – and then donate the cash.

Insurance

Life insurance can be a useful tool for your estate planning. This is especially the case if you have a spouse or children. If you die, you want to make sure they have enough financial resources to continue their standard of living.

A general rule-of-thumb is to have the death benefit – which is the amount paid to your beneficiaries – at least ten times your income. But of course, everyone's situation is different. What if you have a lot of debt? Or you want to make sure you have enough money for college for your children?

Insurance companies do have online calculators to make estimates. You can also seek advice from a financial planner or insurance agent.

There are two main types of insurance:

- Term Insurance: This is for a fixed period of time, say 20, 25, or 30 years. This is pure insurance since – when it expires – there is no more coverage or cash value. Purchasing a new policy will usually be at higher premiums. This is why you want to make sure the duration of your policy is long enough. One approach is that it should last for the number of years that your youngest child will reach age 18.

- Permanent Insurance: This includes whole life, universal life, variable life, and variable universal life. These policies provide coverage for your entire life, so long as you maintain the premium payments. There is also a cash value. This is the part of your premiums that grow tax-free. Depending on your policy, this may be the result of interest or even stock investments. You can borrow against the cash value, or surrender the whole amount, which can result in hefty fees.

In many cases, term insurance is the right one. It has the most coverage for the price.

However, there are cases where a permanent policy makes sense (note that you can purchase a term policy that converts into permanent insurance). For example, you might have a child that has special needs who requires life-long support. Or a permanent insurance policy can be a way to pay for estate taxes. This is so long as you use an insurance trust.

Note   As your wealth grows, you could be vulnerable to lawsuits. Simply put, your auto and homeowners' policies may not be sufficient protection. Because of this, you might want to consider an umbrella policy. This is often for those with net worths over $2 million.

Digital Assets

For your estate, a large proportion of the value could be from digital assets like crypto, PayPal accounts, NFTs, domain names, and so on. Or some of the assets may have sentimental value, such as your online photo albums on your smartphone.

So, what happens to these assets when you die? It depends on the laws of your state. But it is a good idea to use a vault to itemize your digital assets, indicate the locations of any documents, and passwords. You can provide access to your heirs and include the details in your estate documents.

Note   You might think that keeping your estate planning documents in a safety deposit box is a good idea. However, this may cause more problems. Keep in mind that your heirs may need a court order to access it – which can be time-consuming.

Updates and Advice

The laws and regulations of estate planning change frequently. Of course, they can be very complex. As a result, it is usually a good idea to hire an expert. This person is usually a licensed attorney.

You should also periodically review your estate plan. This is especially the case if there have been major life changes, such as a marriage, the birth of a child, divorce, and so on. Some of the biggest problems with estate planning are due to not making the necessary changes in your life.

Finally, it is important to communicate. When it comes to estate planning, there is always the risk of causing problems with your family. Some may feel left out or even cheated. So as much as possible, try to get a sense of how your family may feel.

Conclusion

When it comes to estate planning, the best time to start is now. Having a will, the necessary healthcare documents, and the right beneficiaries' designations can help to avoid many problems. You might also want to explore getting a trust as well as a digital vault. Then there is life insurance, which can be essential for making sure you provide for your family.

Okay then, we are now at the end of the book. We have certainly covered a lot. But do not feel overwhelmed. Again, you can use this book as a reference. When you have a certain issue, you can go to the particular chapter for some help.

You should also seek professional advice. Financial matters are challenging, and you do not want to make any major mistakes. A professional advisor can be an invaluable guide.

So then, good luck on your tech journey!

Index

A

© Tom Taulli 2022
T. Taulli, *The Personal Finance Guide for Tech Professionals*,
https://doi.org/10.1007/978-1-4842-8242-7

Printed in the United States
by Baker & Taylor Publisher Services

Printed in the United States
by Baker & Taylor Publisher Services